VAN GOGH SUNFLOWERS

MARTIN GAYFORD

National Gallery Global, London
Distributed by Yale University Press

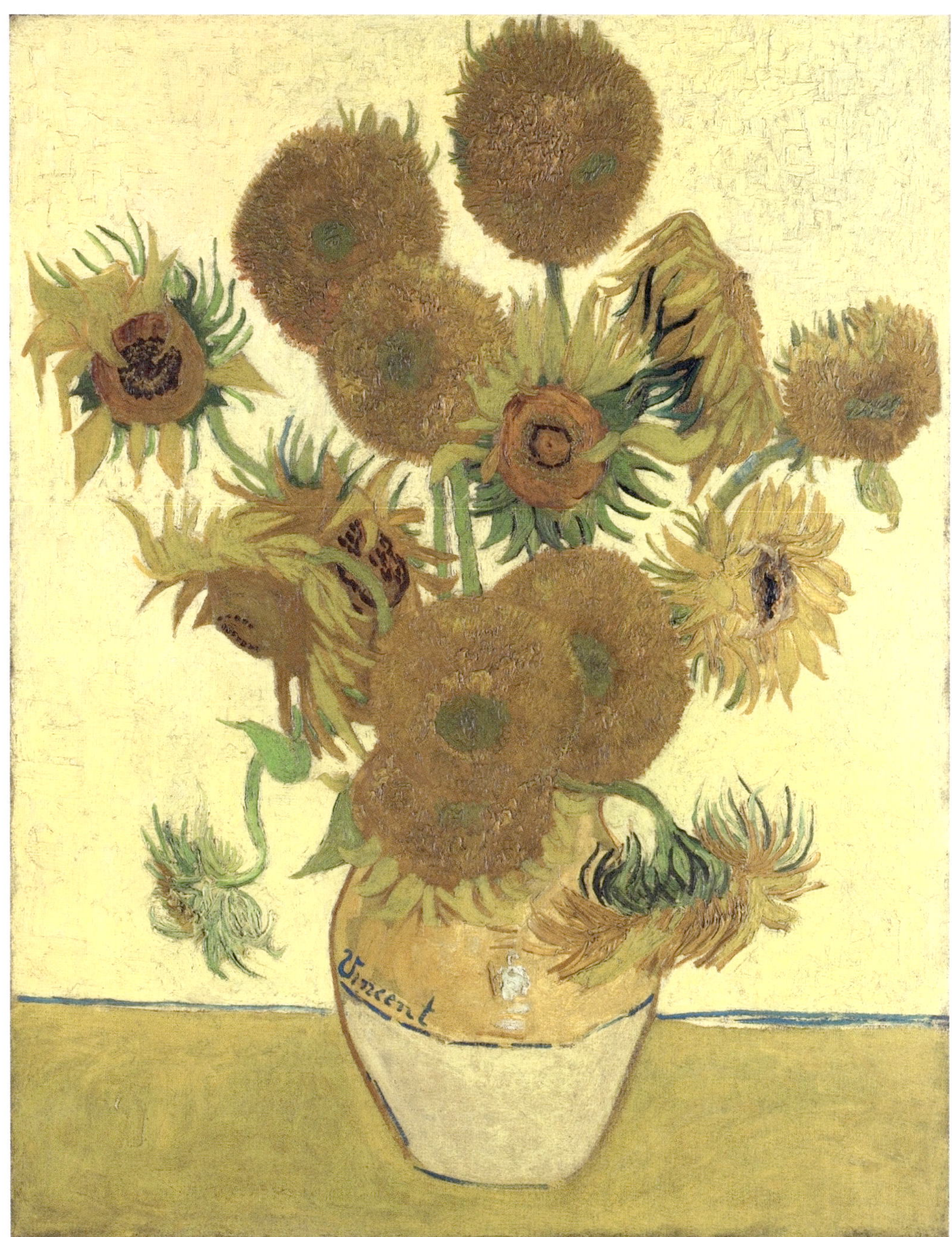
Vincent

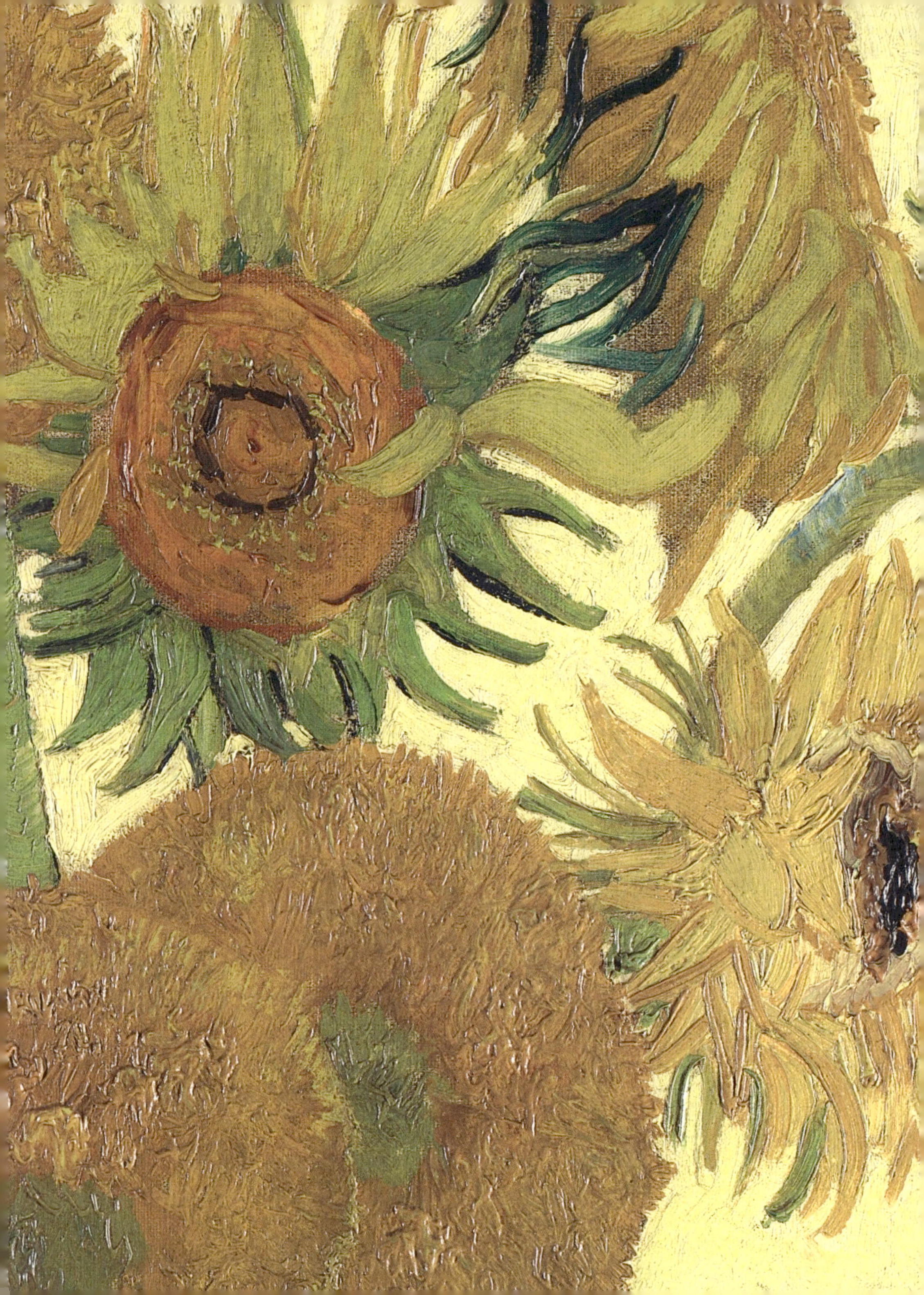

1 *Sunflowers*, 1888
Oil on canvas, 92.1×73 cm
The National Gallery, London

THE PAINTER OF SUNFLOWERS

Early in December 1888, Paul Gauguin painted a portrait of his then housemate, Vincent van Gogh. It is a strange work, in which it is hard to recognise the face familiar from Van Gogh's many self portraits. He is seen from above while working on a canvas, which is turned away from the viewer (fig. 2). But it is not hard to guess the subject since Vincent is directing his half-closed eyes not at the picture he is painting, but at a bunch of yellow and orange sunflowers in a majolica vase, balanced on a rush-bottomed chair to his left.

When the portrait was finished, Gauguin offered it as a gift to Vincent's younger brother Theo. He wrote self-deprecatingly: 'From the geographical point of view, perhaps, it is not a very good likeness, but I think it does convey something of his inner character and, if you have no objection, keep it, unless you do not like it.'[1] Although his tone was casual, this was an important matter to Gauguin; at that point Theo van Gogh was the only dealer in his art and his main financial support. Vincent, in turn, was extremely close to Theo. It follows that Gauguin must have exerted himself to create something remarkable in this picture, an image that captured what was most unusual and characteristic in his sitter.

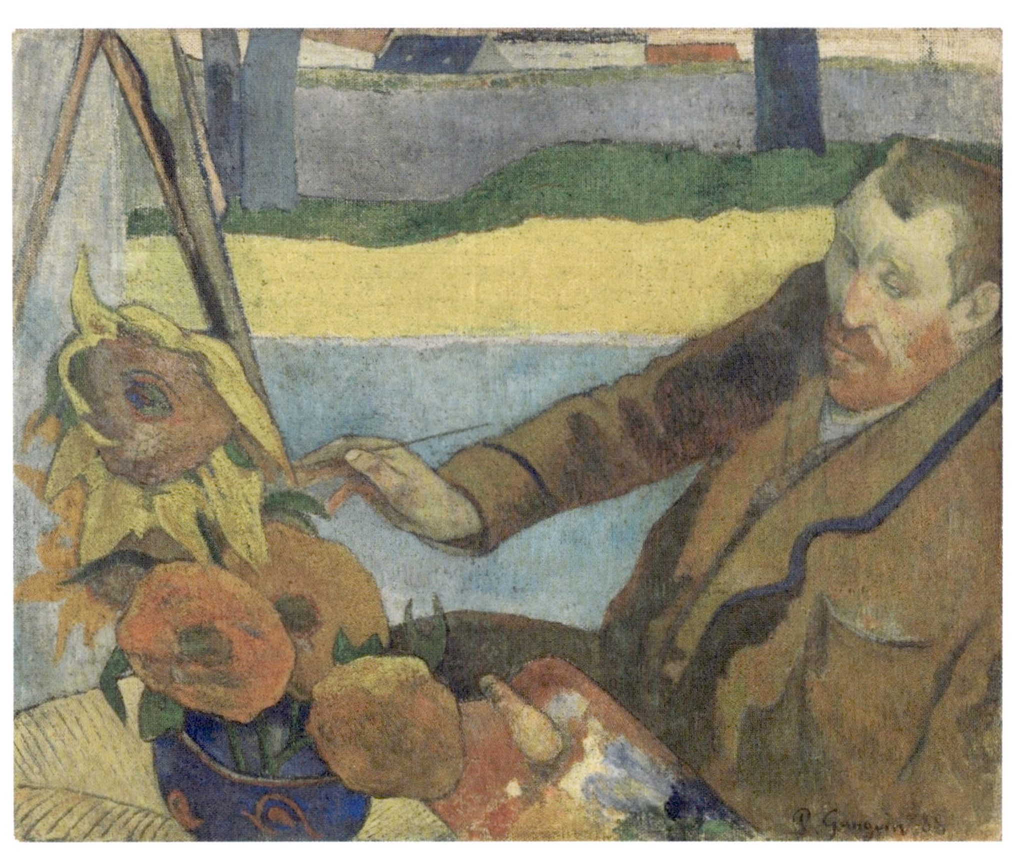

2 Paul Gauguin (1848–1903)
Vincent van Gogh painting Sunflowers, 1888
Oil on canvas, 73×91 cm
Van Gogh Museum, Amsterdam (Vincent van Gogh Foundation)

As far as Theo was concerned, he succeeded. On 3 January 1889, just a few weeks after the portrait was made, Theo wrote to his fiancée Jo Bonger, with words of the highest praise: 'It is a great work of art & the best portrait that's been made of him in terms of capturing his inner being.'[2] The way Gauguin did this was both revealing and carefully chosen.

He had portrayed Van Gogh engaged in depicting what he regarded as his most characteristic subject. Towards the end of November 1888, a week or two before this portrait was begun, Vincent reported a flattering remark that had been made in conversation: 'Gauguin was telling me the other day – that he'd seen a painting by Claude Monet of sunflowers in a large Japanese vase, very fine. But – he likes mine better' [721] (fig. 3). On another occasion, talking about Vincent's rendition, Gauguin had exclaimed, almost lost for words: 'that – ... that's ... the flower' [741], meaning, presumably, that Van Gogh had captured its essence.

As we shall see, Gauguin already knew about – and owned – paintings of sunflowers by Van Gogh before he joined him in Arles that October. In a way, these pictures had helped to initiate their friendship. But the paintings Gauguin must have had in mind as he worked on his portrait were the two large canvases hanging in his small bedroom upstairs.

In this little rectangular space, Van Gogh had hung five sizeable pictures to welcome his friend when he came to stay. Of these, the most powerful would have been two paintings of sunflowers in a vase. One is of 14 blooms against a light-blue background (now in the Neue Pinakothek, Munich, fig. 4) and the other, of 15 flowers on a yellow ground, is one of the most celebrated possessions of the National Gallery, London (fig. 1).

It was the second of these which burned into Gauguin's memory and imagination. In a dreamily poetic text he wrote (inaccurately but eloquently) of the painting beside which he fell asleep and rose each morning for two months:

Overleaf:
3 Claude Monet (1840–1926)
Bouquet of Sunflowers, 1881
Oil on canvas, 101×81.3 cm
The Metropolitan Museum of Art, New York. H.O. Havemeyer Collection, Bequest of Mrs. H.O. Havemeyer, 1929

4 *Sunflowers*, 1888
Oil on canvas, 92×73 cm
Bayerische Staatsgemälde-sammlungen, Neue Pinakothek, Munich

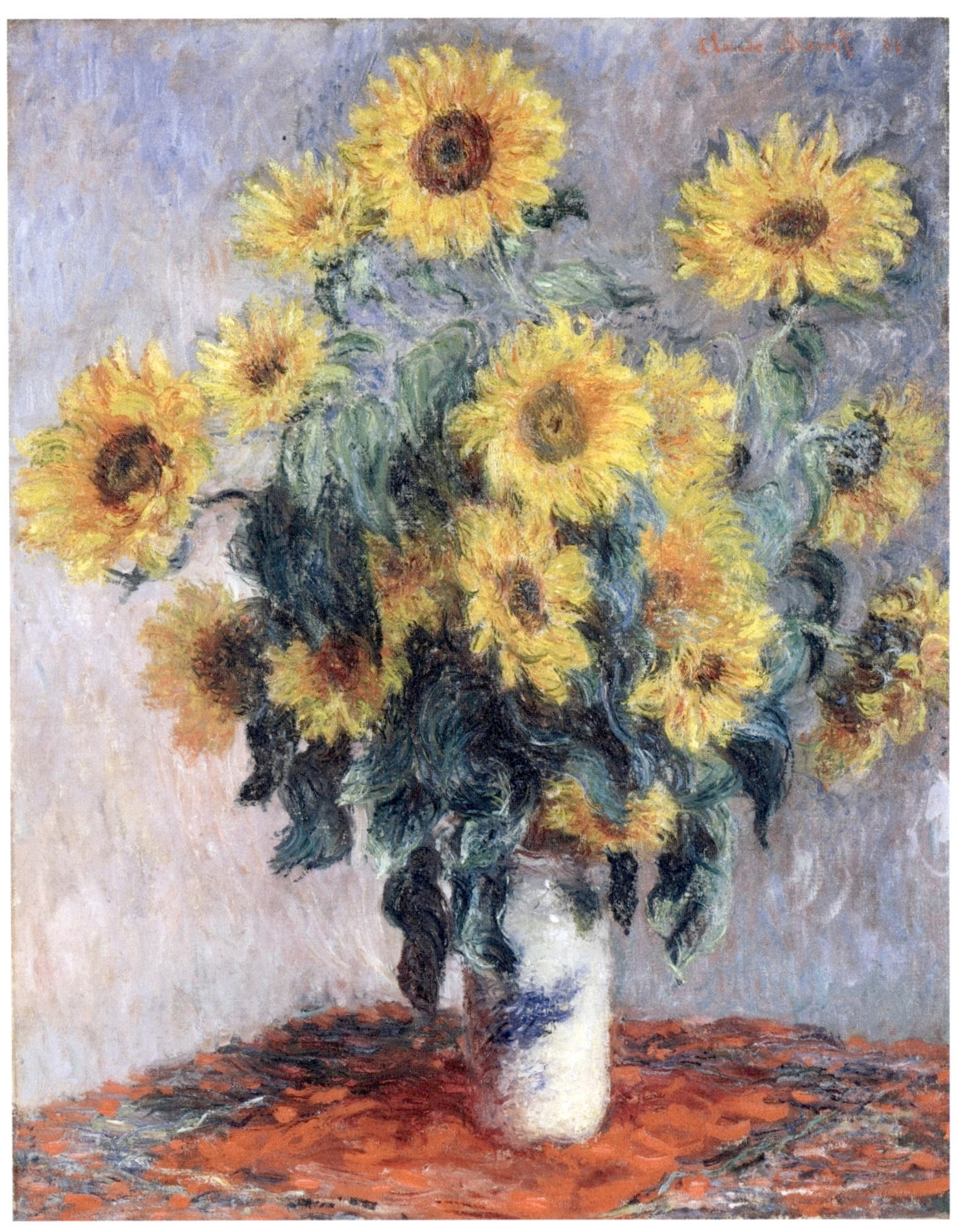

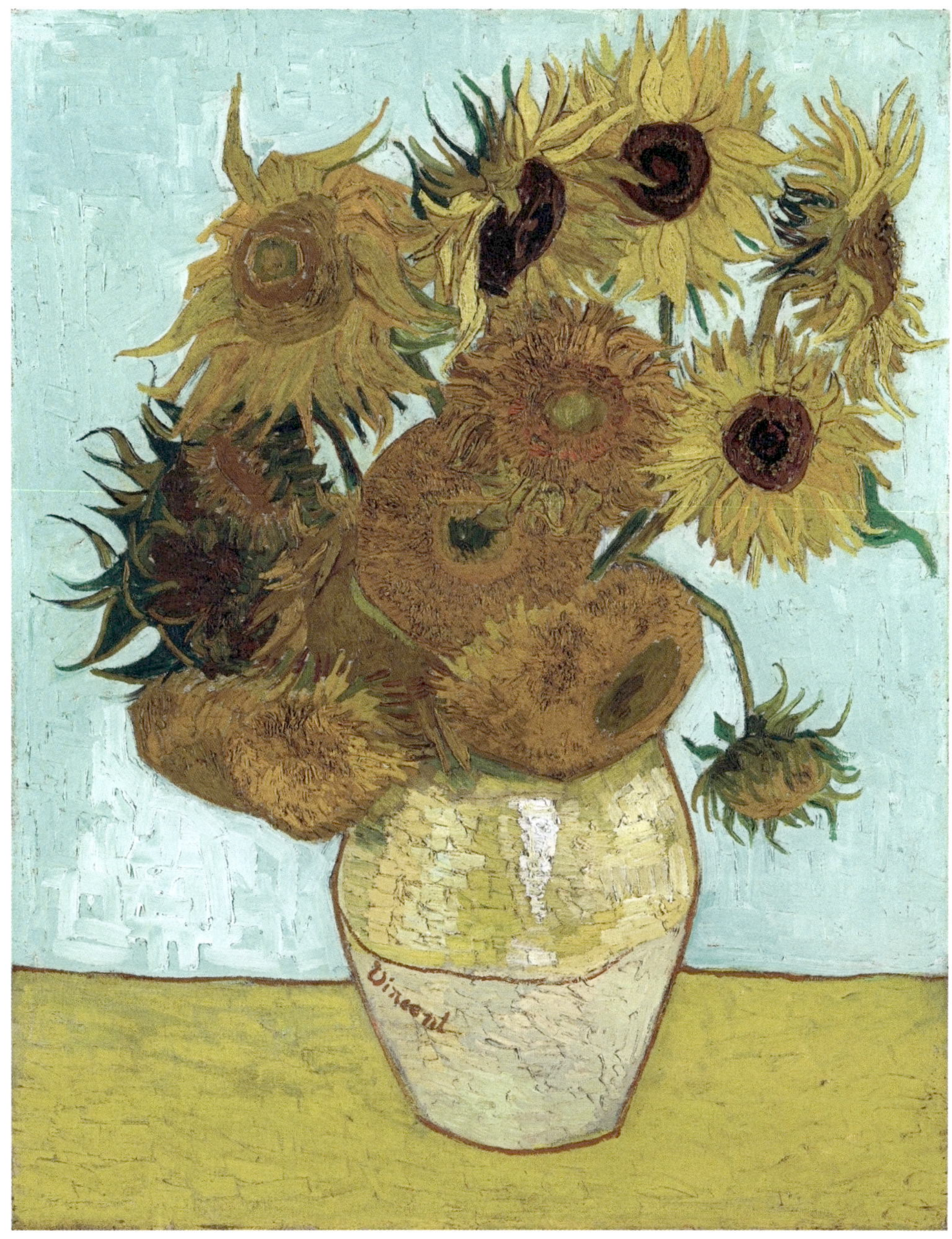
Vincent

> Sunflowers with purple eyes stand out on a yellow background; they bathe their stems in a yellow pot on a yellow table. In a corner of the painting, the signature of the painter: Vincent. And the yellow sun that passes through the yellow curtains of my room floods all this fluorescence with gold; and in the morning upon awakening from my bed, I imagine that all this smells very good.[3]

More straightforwardly, in January 1889, shortly after he left Arles, Gauguin wrote to his old housemate, asking if he would give him the 'sunflowers on a yellow background which I regard as a perfect page of an essential "Vincent" style' [734]. This is, of course, how most art lovers, everywhere, have long thought of this picture. But what was it about Van Gogh's paintings of sunflowers that so impressed Gauguin, who was an older, more experienced artist and an acknowledged leader of the avant-garde? And how was it that Van Gogh came to paint these flowers four times, at astonishing speed, during the summer of 1888? The answers to these questions are the subject of this book.

AS IMMENSELY CHEERFUL AS HOLLAND IS SAD[4]

In Provence the summer of 1888 was a bad one. It was torridly hot, which was normal. But there was also an unusual mistral, a persistent northerly wind that became turbocharged as it blew down the Rhône valley. That year the mistral appeared in midsummer, when it was normally strongest in spring and winter. Naturally, the people of Arles grumbled.

For his part, Van Gogh luxuriated in the sun, although sometimes it left him 'dazed' [644]. The heat and light of southern France were two of the factors that had lured him down from Paris the previous February. In his opinion, a person from the cold, dark north of Europe could not get enough of either. Paris, where he had lived for the previous two years, was an improvement on his earlier life in the Netherlands,

5 *Arles: View from the Wheatfields*, 1888
Reed and quill pens and brown ink on paper, 31.2×24.1 cm
J. Paul Getty Museum, Los Angeles

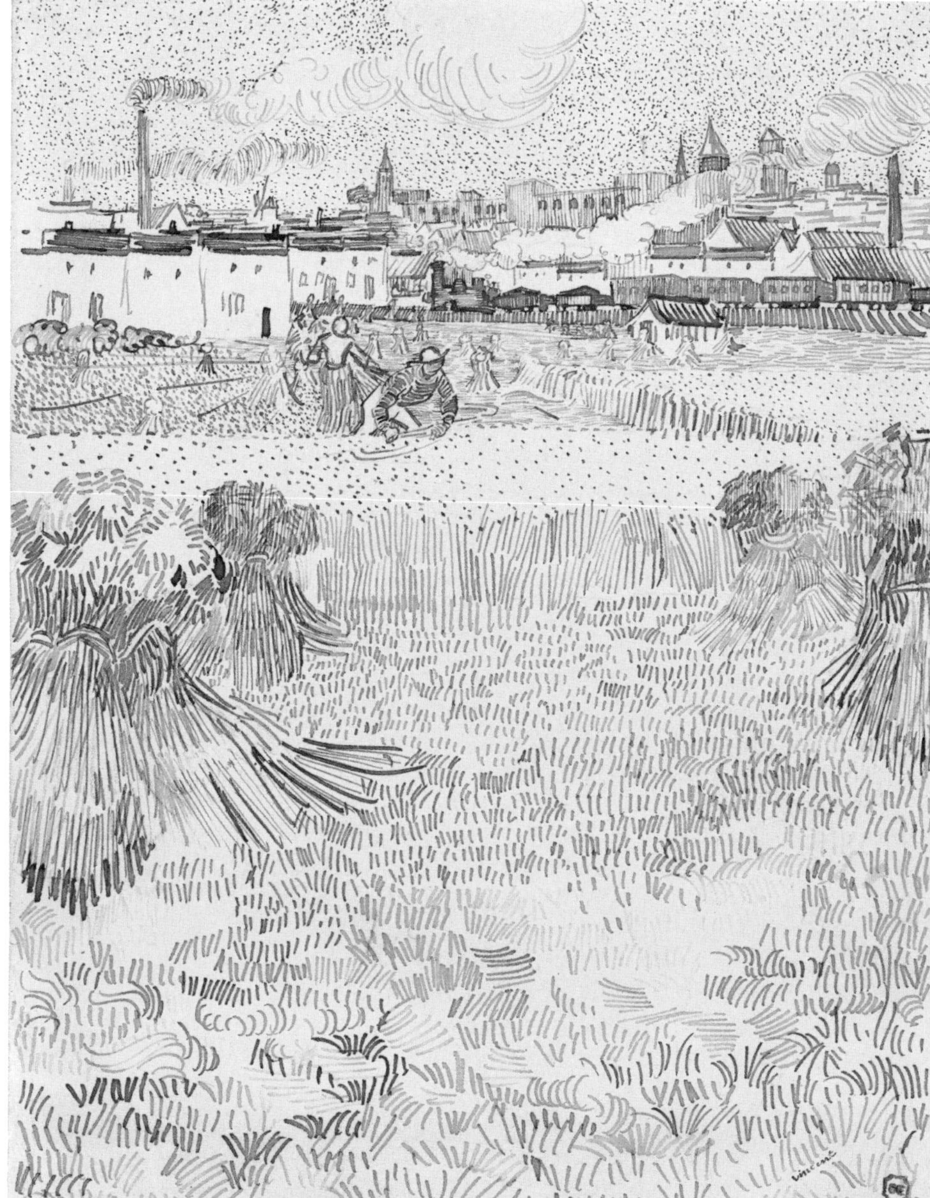

but still not southerly enough. The sun, he believed, 'has never sufficiently penetrated us northerners' [678].

The mistral, however, was another matter. This was, he wrote to his youngest sister Willemien, 'a very nasty, nagging wind' [653]. To a painter such as Vincent, who did a great deal of work outdoors (fig. 5), the mistral posed tiresome practical problems, notably, he explained to her, when he had to 'lay my canvas flat on the ground and work on my knees' because his easel did not 'stand firm'. It may have been this constant gale, together with the other difficulties of working in the countryside – such as being 'eaten up by the mosquitoes' [639] – that led him to start looking for subjects less awkward to depict.

At any rate, towards the end of July he began to work much closer to home and in more sheltered conditions. He succeeded in persuading several locals to pose for portraits, which was often a problem for Van Gogh, since his manner and eccentric personality made many people nervous. Another subject he found was gardens, which were walled and thus at least a little protected from the scything wind, and probably not too far from his own lodgings and studio on the outskirts of the town.

These were not only locations in which it would be easier to work; at that time of year large numbers of brilliantly coloured flowers were in bloom. In a letter to Willemien of 31 July, Vincent described one of these canvases in terms which were more or less equally chromatic and horticultural:

> Poppies and other red flowers in green in the foreground, then a patch of *blue*bells. Then a patch of orange and yellow African marigolds, then white and yellow flowers and finally, in the background, pink and lilac and also scabious, dark violet, and red geraniums and sunflowers and a fig tree and oleander and a vine. At the end, black cypresses against little low white houses with orange roofs – and a delicate green-blue strip of sky. [653]

The equation flower = colour was clear enough in this description. Van Gogh immediately confessed that he had in fact reduced each bloom to a mark of his brush: 'I know very well that not a single flower was drawn, that they're just little licks of colour, red, yellow, orange, green, blue, violet, but the impression of all those colours against one another is nonetheless there in the painting as it is in nature.' But then, instantly, his confidence began to ebb. 'I imagine it would disappoint you and appear ugly were you to see it.' Nonetheless, he hoped his sister would agree that 'the motif is really summery' (fig. 6).

He painted a second picture of this garden, which belonged to a farmhouse, even more radical and extreme than the other (fig. 7). In this – which was in a vertical, 'portrait' format – the flowers had been reduced, exactly as he had written to Willemien, to 'just little licks of colour' – but more so than in the other picture, because the viewpoint was closer. In cinematic terms, Vincent had tracked in so that the painting was largely filled by horizonal bands of flowers, almost stripes: red poppies in the foreground, above them blue flowers flecked with yellow, then, orange, mauve, orange – and small in the distance a more naturalistic touch, the white farmhouse.

On the right – rather oversized and perhaps added later to prevent any possible sense of monotony in this picture, which otherwise consisted of a mass of stripes and pulsating, vivid dots – he added a spray of tall sunflowers. These huge blooms were to occupy his thoughts over the weeks to come. Before a month had passed he had made them the subject of masterpieces yet more extraordinary and extreme than these paintings of a Provençal garden.

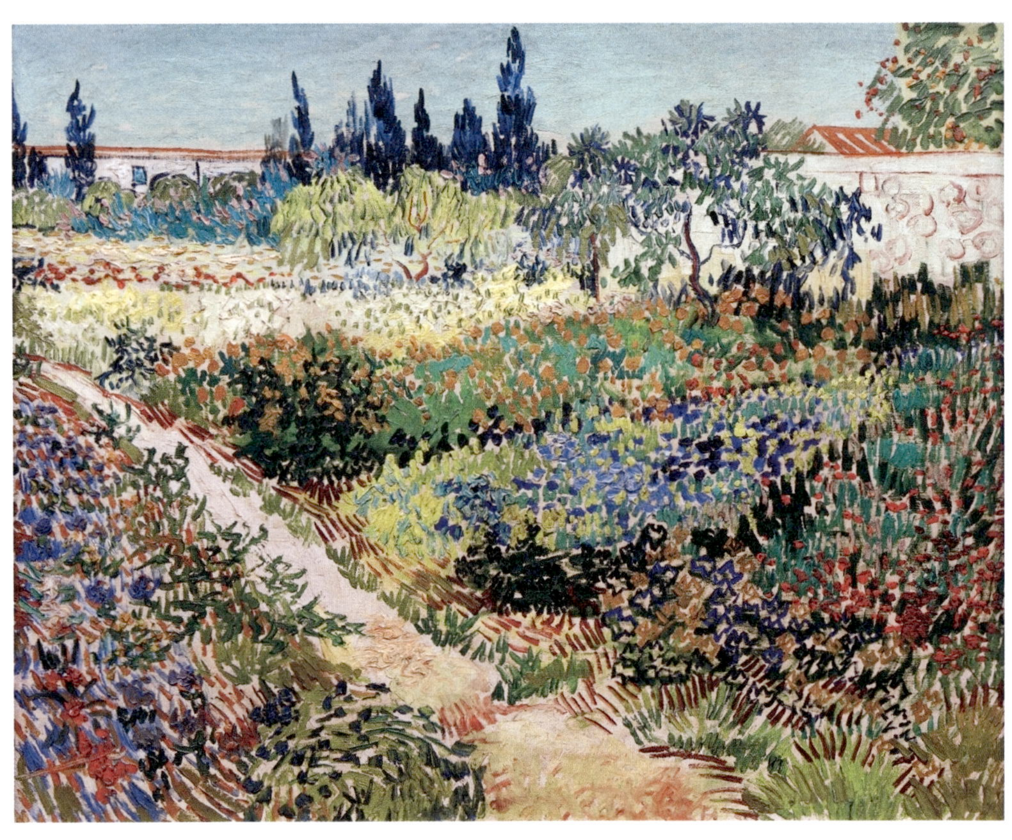

6 *Garden at Arles*, 1888
Oil on canvas, 73×92 cm
Kunstmuseum Den Haag

7 *Garden with Flowers*, 1888
Oil on canvas, 92×73 cm
Private collection

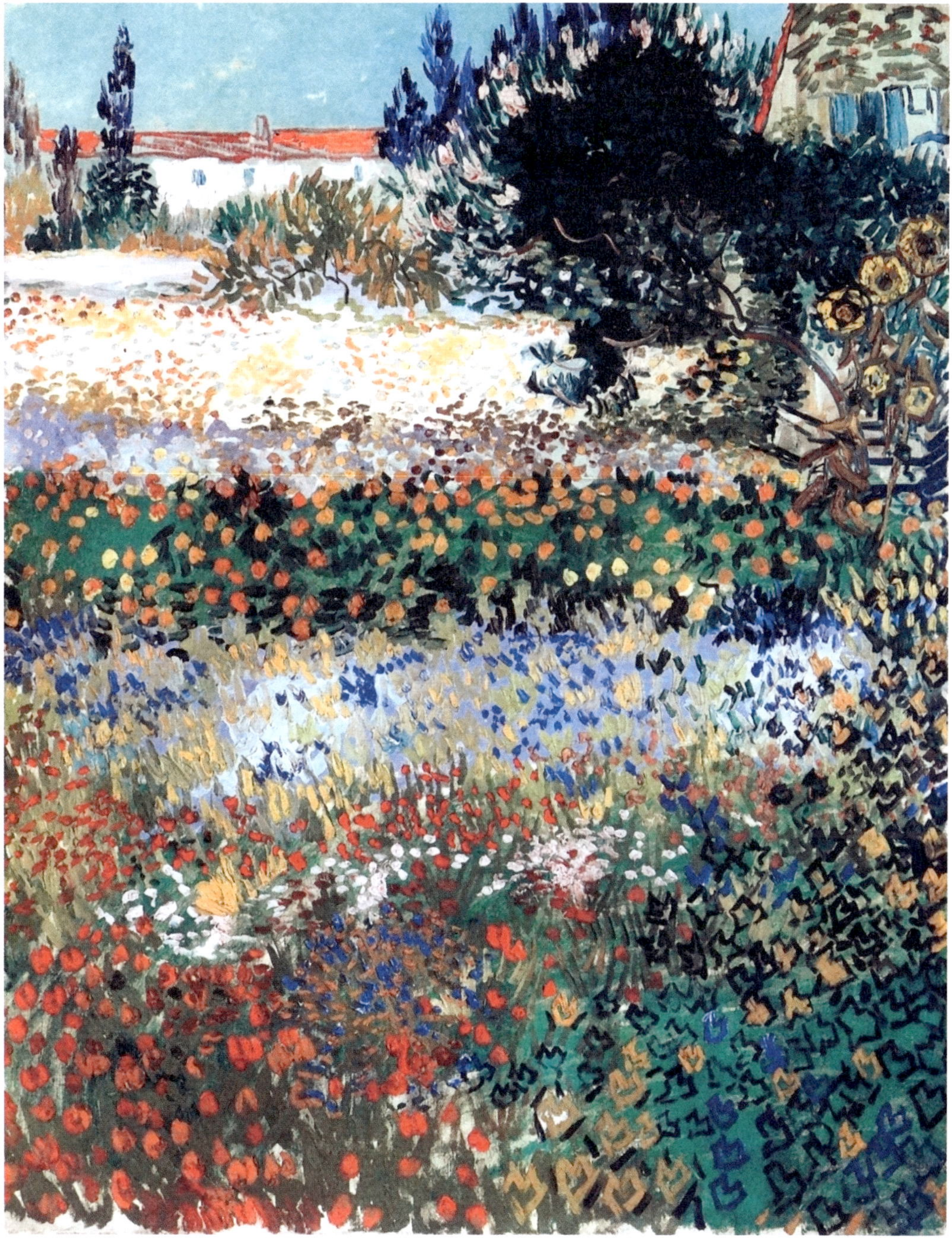

THE QUESTION OF COLOUR[5]

In the summer of 1888 Van Gogh, who had just turned 35, had been an artist for almost eight years. Born in March 1853, he had led a life remarkable for its variety of occupation, location and – as far as an outside observer could judge – lack of achievement.

Van Gogh decided to become a painter in August 1880 and immediately began to draw and study. Previously, he had been an utter failure in a series of endeavours. In order, he had been an art dealer, unpaid assistant master in a preparatory school in Ramsgate, Kent, teacher at a school in Isleworth, West London, sales assistant in a bookshop, would-be theology student (unable to gain entrance to university), and a volunteer, unsalaried lay preacher in the Belgian coalfields.

At this point no one, and certainly not his despairing and long-suffering parents, would have predicted that within a relatively short number of years he would produce drawings and paintings that would be hailed as works of genius. On the contrary, they regarded him as a hopeless and pitiable case, 'a cross we must bear'.[6] Something ailed Van Gogh, and perhaps had done so since childhood. Exactly what has long been debated; it was possibly a form of bipolar disorder and/or some epileptic condition (there is no reason why he should have suffered from only one affliction).

Whatever Vincent's problem was, his father the Reverend Theodorus van Gogh, a pastor of the Dutch Reformed Church, concluded that his eccentricity amounted to mental illness. Early in 1880, Theodorus summoned a family council to agree to have his 27-year-old son sent to a psychiatric hospital at a village in Belgium called Geel – in Vincent's words, 'to pack me off to a madhouse' [228]. He resisted his parents' well-intentioned plans 'with all my might' [185].

Instead, he decided to become an artist (fig. 8). In this new career Vincent's progress, though not noticed by many people except his brother Theo, was astonishingly rapid. For five years he worked in various parts of the Netherlands. Then,

8 *Self Portrait*, 1887
Oil on artist's board, mounted on cradled panel, 41×32.5 cm
The Art Institute of Chicago. Joseph Winterbotham Collection

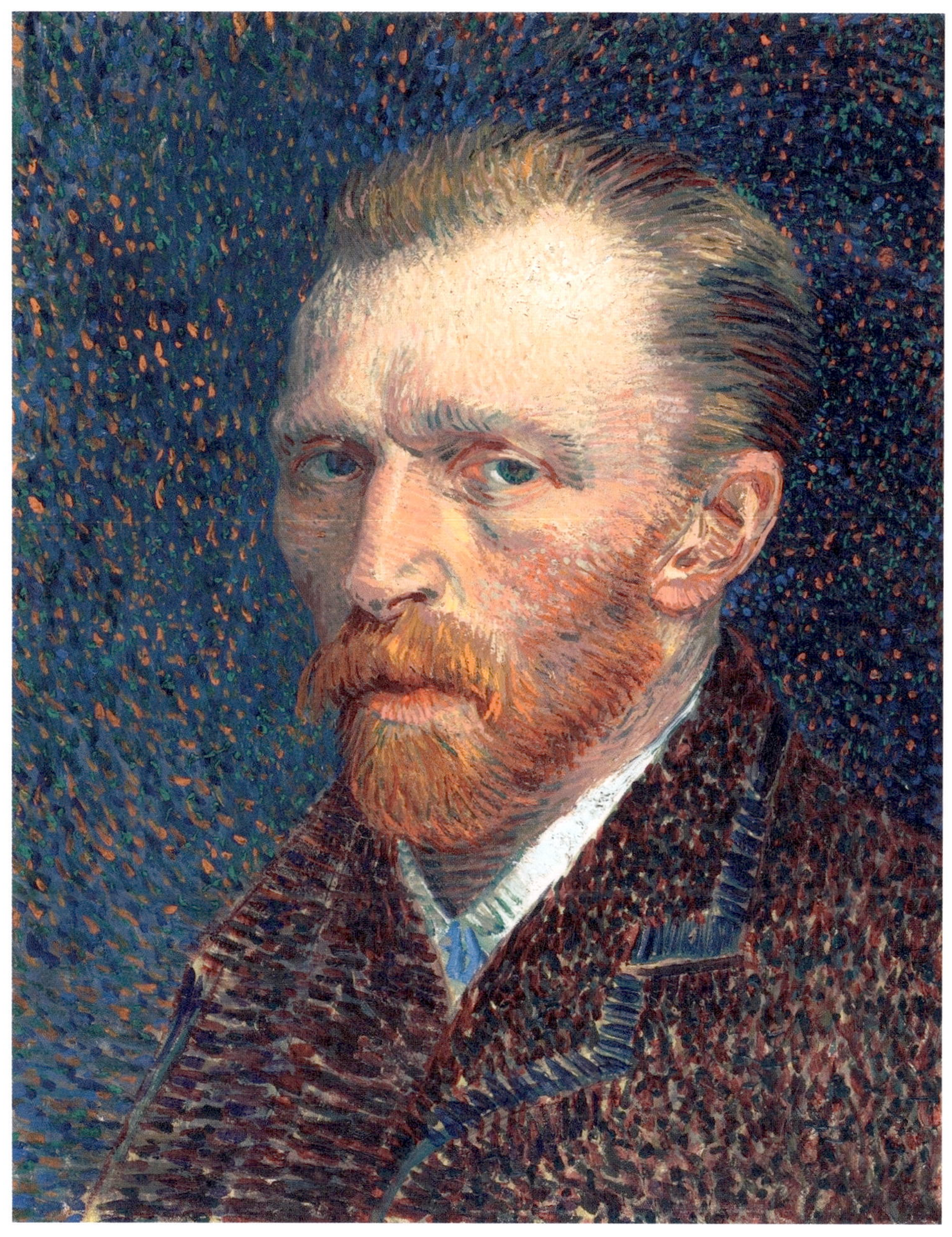

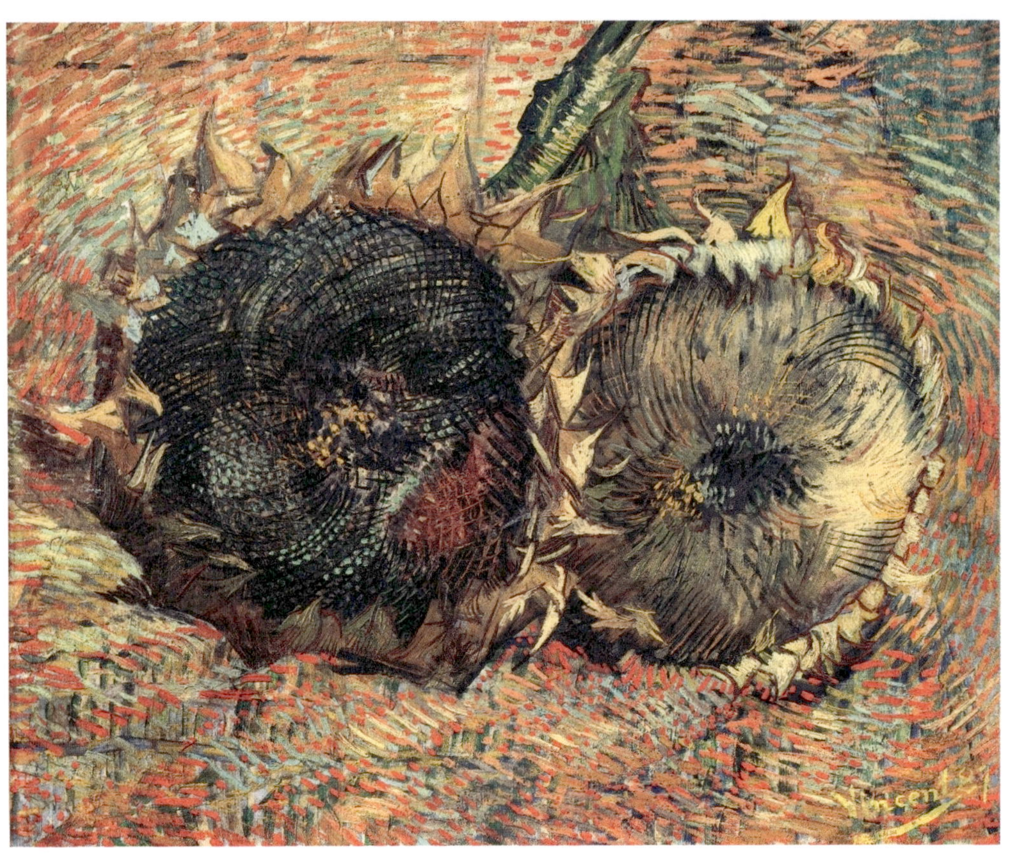

9 *Sunflowers*, 1887
Oil on canvas, 50 × 60.7 cm
Museum of Fine Arts Bern, Gift of Prof. Dr Hans R. Hahnloser, Bern, 1971

after his father's death and a short sojourn in Antwerp, in March 1886 he turned up in Paris, to Theo's surprise – and perhaps dismay. It was Theo who provided Vincent with money, painting and drawing equipment, praise and advice. There are signs, however, that he found Vincent difficult company now that they had to interact in person rather than at a distance. Ostensibly, Theo had succeeded where his elder brother had failed. He had joined the art-dealing business Goupil & Cie, in which one of their uncles was a partner, and prospered in this job. In 1884 he had been transferred to the firm's Paris office, where he continued to do well.

If Vincent had remained in the Netherlands, as David Hockney has observed, twenty-first-century art lovers might still know his name, but we would probably think of him only as an interesting Dutch painter of the late nineteenth century.[7] It was after Van Gogh moved to Paris that he became an artist of world importance. What he discovered there, in a word, was *colour*.

He had previously been aware that some artists loosely described as 'Impressionist' had been doing remarkable things involving daringly bright hues and chromatic contrasts. While he was an inhabitant of Parisian bohemia during the rest of 1886 and through 1887, Van Gogh found out exactly what that meant. He absorbed the lessons of the Impressionists, and also the even more vaguely connected 'Post-Impressionists', including Gauguin and Georges Seurat. And this new chromatic inspiration was supercharged by what he had learnt about how much could be accomplished with the stroke of a brush from his study of Dutch and Flemish predecessors, such as Rembrandt, Peter Paul Rubens and Frans Hals.

Sunflowers appeared in Van Gogh's Parisian work as he explored what the British artist Patrick Heron has called the 'continent' of colour.[8] They peep out from, or tower over, landscapes he painted of the then-rural slopes of Montmartre and they feature in a still life of a bunch of flowers; then, in late August or early September 1887, he produced a quartet of pictures in which sunflowers star, precursors to the masterpieces he produced the following year in Arles.

These Paris sunflowers were not pictures of gardens, nor of bouquets in vases, but detailed *portraits* of individual blooms (fig. 9). Van Gogh wrote of how much he admired the way Japanese artists could make profound art from the smallest details of nature:

> If we study Japanese art, then we see a man, undoubtedly wise and a philosopher and intelligent, who spends his time - on what? - studying the distance from the earth to the moon? - no; studying Bismarck's politics? - no, he studies a single blade of grass. But this blade of grass leads him to draw all the plants - then the seasons, the broad features of landscapes, finally animals, and then the human figure. He spends his life like that, and life is too short to do everything. [686]

In this way Van Gogh discovered hidden worlds within a single sunflower. Although most of us think of its blooms as 'flowers', botanically speaking each one is a 'flower head' (pseudanthium) made up of numerous individual flowers. The larger ones around the outer ring fuse together to resemble petals, while the interior is made up of many small, five-petalled florets. These are packed together in a geometrically intricate arrangement of intersecting spirals, some rotating to the left and others to the right.

The effect is extraordinary: two expanding whorls moving in opposite directions, a miniature solar system. Van Gogh captured this dynamic patterning. He also surrounded the two flower heads with a force-field of short brushstrokes, curved and undulating in contrasting and complementary colours so that the whole canvas thrums with energy.

On another canvas almost the same size as the first, Van Gogh then depicted two flower heads, one turned with its back to the viewer (fig. 10). This time he paid more attention to the colour of the blooms: their orange-yellowness. He accentuated this by putting them on a ground of light and dark blues, flecked with touches of yellow and purple.

Perhaps when painting these pictures he had in mind an exhibition that would take place later in the autumn. The location was, his friend Emile Bernard recalled, 'the dining-room of a working-class restaurant' (to be precise, the Grand Bouillon-Restaurant du Chalet on avenue de Clichy) and was 'an endeavour on Van Gogh's part alone'.[9] He showed numerous works; others exhibiting included Bernard, Henri de Toulouse-Lautrec and Louis Anquetin – all young, experimental artists whom Van Gogh dubbed the painters of the 'Petit Boulevard', as opposed to the older, more established but still innovatory figures such as Monet and Edgar Degas. The 'little boulevard' was the boulevard de Clichy, where Seurat and Paul Signac had their studios and off which the avenue de Clichy branches.

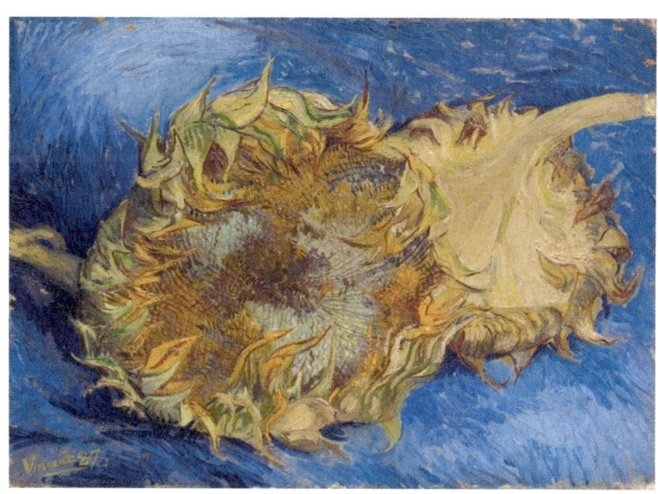

10 *Sunflowers*, 1887
Oil on canvas, 43.2×61 cm
The Metropolitan Museum of Art, New York. Rogers Fund, 1949

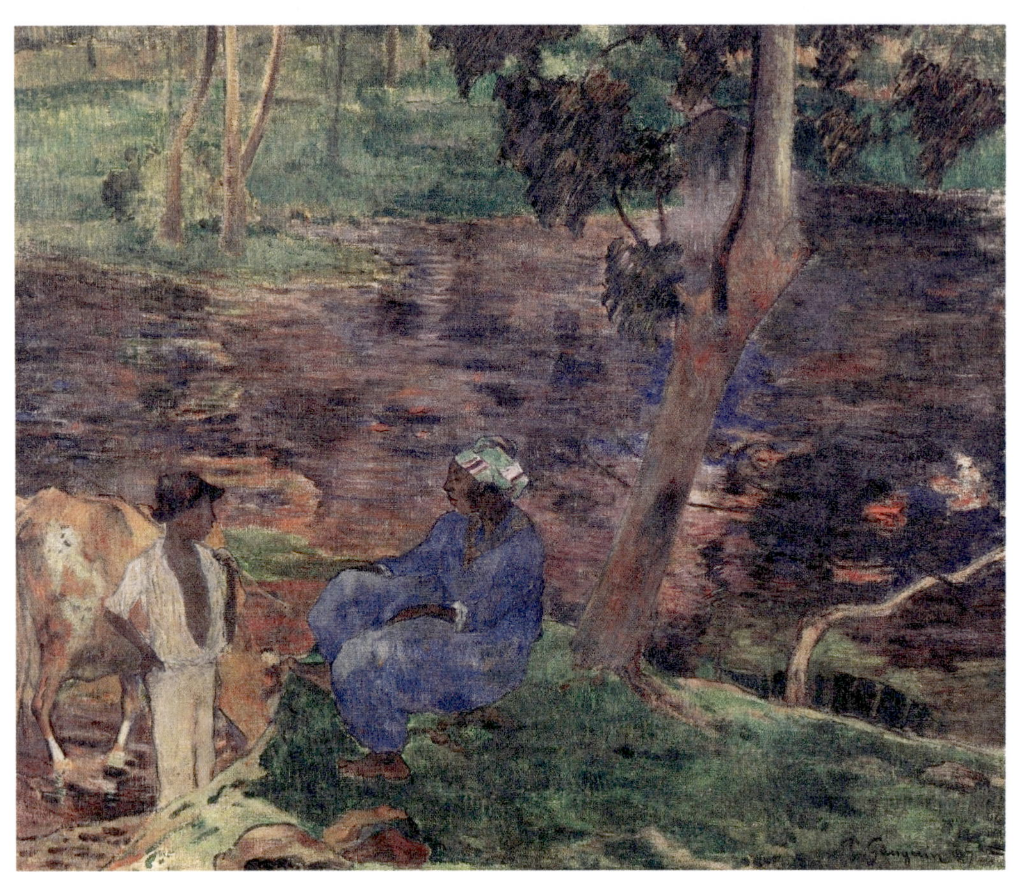

11 Paul Gauguin (1848–1903)
On the Banks of the River, Martinique, 1887
Oil on canvas, 54.5×65.5 cm
Van Gogh Museum, Amsterdam (Vincent van Gogh Foundation)

This exhibition was scarcely a success. None of the participants sold much and Van Gogh nothing at all. Eventually, according to Bernard, Van Gogh had 'a violent altercation' with the owner 'which made Vincent decide to take a hand-barrow without delay and cart the whole exhibition to his studio'.[10] He did, however, make a crucial contact with one visitor: Paul Gauguin.

The latter had been on the other side of the Atlantic since the previous April, enduring difficult and impoverished conditions in Panama and Martinique. He returned to France on 14 November 1887, after working his passage as a seaman. At this date Gauguin was approaching 40, having been a late starter as a full-time artist. Back home he found himself worryingly short of cash – and also in need of allies and supporters after quarrelling with several other members of the avant-garde.

He found two hugely enthusiastic new admirers in the brothers Van Gogh and arranged an exchange of work with Vincent in December. They agreed that Vincent would give him the two paintings of cut sunflowers, and in return Gauguin would give him one of the pictures he had painted in the Caribbean, *On the Banks of the River, Martinique* (fig. 11).

THE RUSTIC SUNFLOWER[11]

The following summer in Arles, sunflowers continued to be on Van Gogh's mind in the days after he had completed the two paintings, plus several drawings, of the farmhouse garden. He found a further subject in 'the little garden of a bathhouse' [657]. This seems to have been situated at 38 rue de Vers – just over the old town wall from his lodgings and studio on place Lamartine – and was located in the red-light district. The brothels and the women who worked there were often in his thoughts, for reasons partly sexual and partly artistic. Bernard, who was obsessed with the idea of the brothel, its staff and customers as a subject for pictures, sent Van Gogh numerous drawings and poems on this theme.

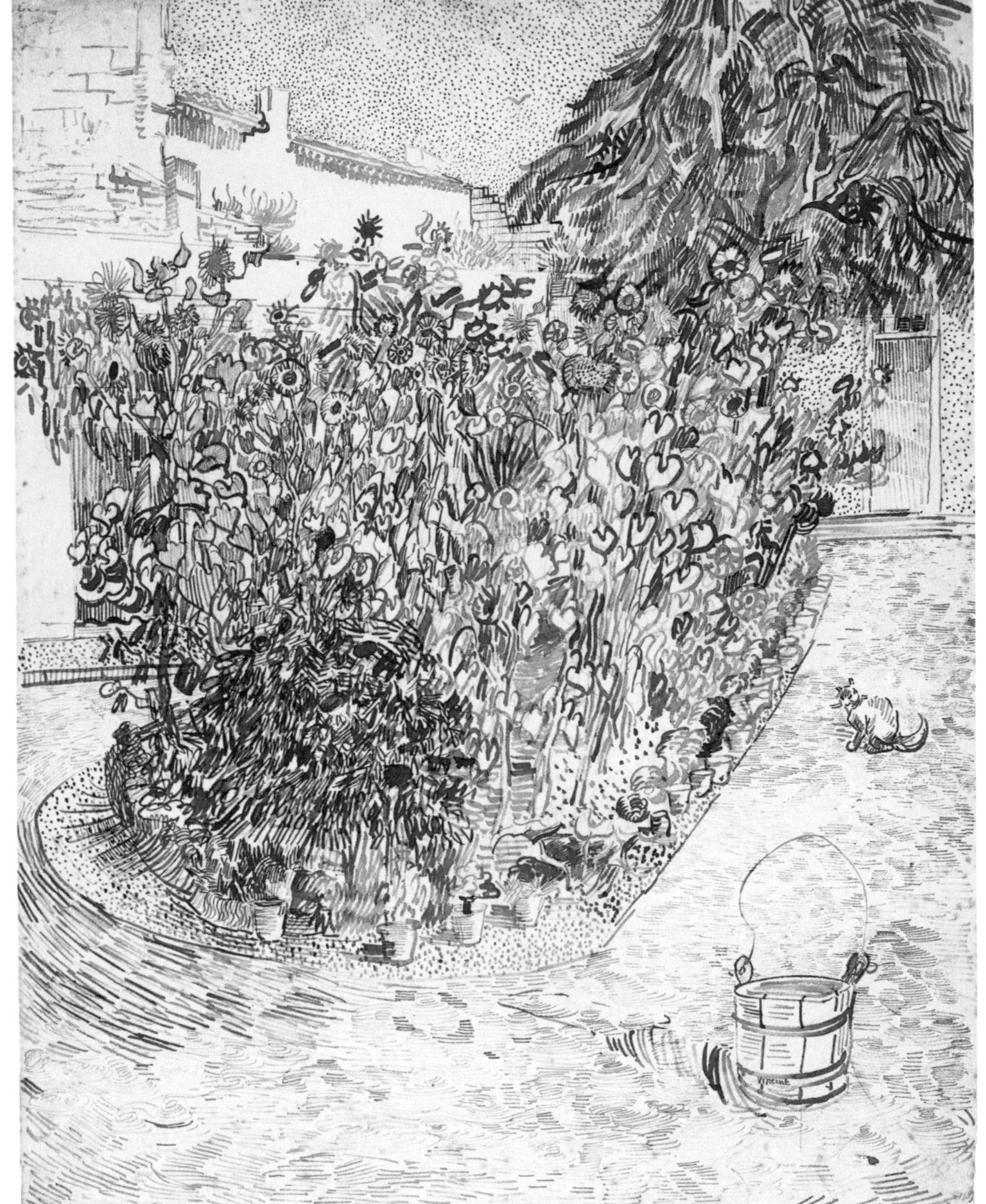

12 *Garden of a Bathhouse*, 1888
Pencil, reed pen, brush and ink on paper, 60.7 × 49.2 cm
Van Gogh Museum, Amsterdam (Vincent van Gogh Foundation)

The gardens of Provence, it seemed to Vincent, exuded an amorous aura. He explained as much to Theo in a letter of 8 August: 'Under the blue sky, the orange, yellow, red patches of flowers take on an amazing brilliance, and in the limpid air there's something happier and more suggestive of love than in the north' [657]. With this letter he dispatched three large and beautiful drawings: two of the farmhouse garden and one of this newly discovered garden beside the bathhouse (fig. 12).

This last was never translated into an oil painting. But one can see from the drawing that such a picture would have consisted of a dense thicket of sunflowers, all yellow, orange, ochre and green, framed by buildings, a shading tree, paved courtyard, a bucket and a resting cat. To Van Gogh it doubtless would have seemed that those flowers were sending out powerful vibrations of love and life.

Shortly afterwards, in this same letter to Theo, Vincent announced: 'I'm annoyed with myself for not painting flowers here.' This was followed by a lapse into despondency, which makes surprising reading almost a century and a half later: 'even having already produced about fifty drawings or painted studies here, I feel as though I've done absolutely nothing at all.' The works he wrote off are now, of course, among the best-loved, most famed and valuable in the world. But Van Gogh wanted to go further, faster.

HEAVILY HANGS THE BROAD SUNFLOWER[12]

Sunflowers as a subject were far from novel in the late nineteenth century. During the period 1873–6, much of which Van Gogh spent in Britain, he could scarcely have avoided seeing sunflowers represented in art and architecture. By that date these blooms were to be seen all over London in paintings and drawings, carved in stone, moulded in brick and even cast in bronze. The sunflower was a favourite symbol of the Pre-Raphaelites, the Arts and Crafts revival and the Aesthetic Movement.

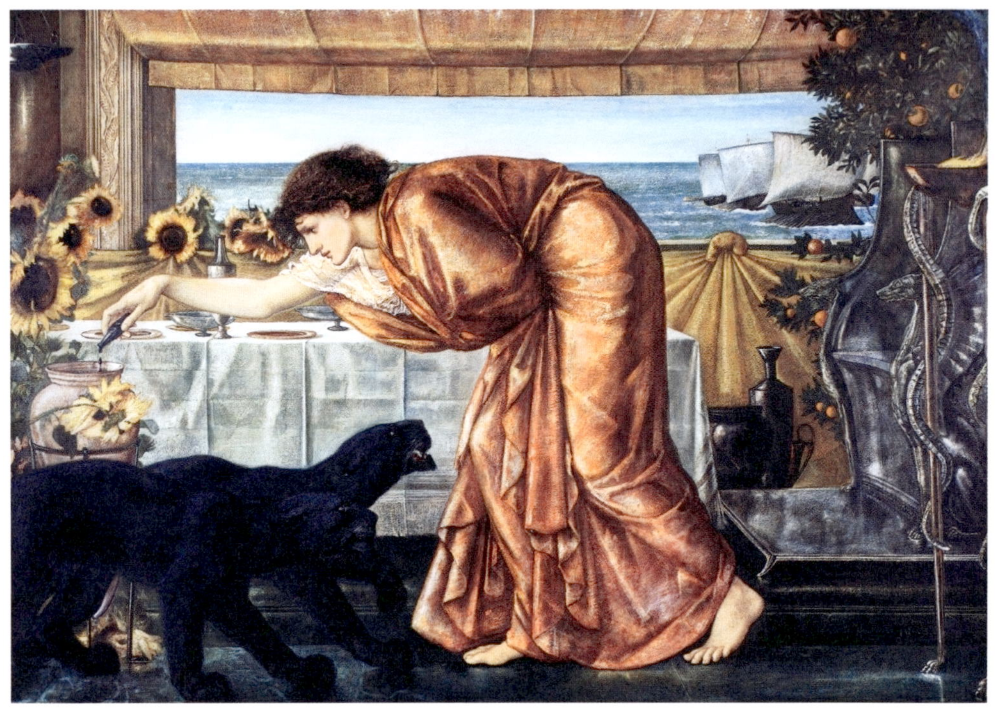

13 Edward Burne-Jones (1833–1898)
The Wine of Circe, 1863–9
Watercolour and bodycolour on paper, 70 × 101.5 cm
Private collection

The first of those, especially, were important predecessors in Vincent's mind. In a letter to Theo of June 1888, during one of many exasperated discussions of his plan to persuade Gauguin to come south and join him in Arles, he broke off to make a comparison. 'You know that I believe that an association of the Impressionists would be something along the lines of the associations of the 12 English Pre-Raphaelites, and that I believe that it could come into being' [625].

This was to be an idealistic commune, in which 'earnings as well as losses would be shared'. Although after an intensely devout phase in his twenties Vincent had lost his faith, artistic and religious ideas still blended in his mind. Perhaps that was why he thought the Pre-Raphaelites numbered 12 – like the Apostles. In reality, there had been just seven members of the Brotherhood.

Ever since they had been transported from the Americas to Europe in the sixteenth century, sunflowers had fired people's imaginations. One reason for this was the (incorrect) belief that their flower heads turn through the day to follow the sun. This led to their being associated with loyalty and devotion. By contrast, these blooms seemed to signify something altogether more erotic to Pre-Raphaelites such as William Morris and Edward Burne-Jones (fig. 13). The latter talked of the flowers as if they were flirting with him: 'Do you know sunflowers? How they peep at you and look brazen sometimes and proud – and others look shy and some so modest that up go their hands to hide their brown blushes.'[13]

The vigorous, ebullient appearance of the sunflower naturally suggested flourishing life, but also – as it withered and drooped – decline and death. Van Gogh constantly made similar connections, sometimes between apparently incompatible objects and ideas. He might well simultaneously have associated these plants with devotion and loyalty, but also the mutual trust and friendship of a band of brother artists, love, sex and the cycle of life and death. Then there were links that only he made.

Looking back the following year, he wrote of the 'high yellow note' [752] he had sustained while painting the fields of wheat at harvest time and the sunflowers. It was as if he thought of it as a sound, like the blast of a trumpet, blown in the utmost register of the instrument.

The incandescent colours in which he painted sunflowers that summer in Arles also stood for Van Gogh himself, and all the frenetic energy and inspiration he poured into his paintings at that time. He made this very point the following January while musing that the sunflower pictures might be good enough to sell: 'to be sufficiently heated up to melt those golds and those flower tones, not just anybody can do that, it takes an individual's whole and entire energy and attention' [741].

BUSY WITH MY SUNFLOWERS[14]

On 21 or 22 August, Vincent wrote to Theo in a state of elation. 'I'm writing to you in great haste', he began, 'to tell you that I've just received a line from Gauguin, who says that he hasn't written because he was doing a great deal of work, but says he's still ready to come to the south as soon as chance permits' [666].

The next item of news was that he had begun a new series of paintings: 'I'm painting with the gusto of a Marseillais eating bouillabaisse, which won't surprise you when it's a question of painting *large* Sunflowers.' He intended to fill the studio where he worked, which was in the little house he rented – later famous as the Yellow House (fig. 14) – with a cycle of pictures that would express the spirit and aspirations of an artistic colony in the Mediterranean south. Although he had been renting the building for some months, up to this point he had been sleeping at the Café de la Gare, which was close by and run by two friends of his, Joseph and Marie Ginoux. Perhaps this seemed easier or less lonely. With the prospect of a housemate, Van Gogh set about furnishing the house and filling it with his work. As he explained: 'In the hope of living in a studio of our own with Gauguin, I'd like to do a decoration for the studio. *Nothing but large Sunflowers*.'

The idea that Gauguin should come to join him in Arles had taken root in his mind months before. But Gauguin, established in Brittany and still recovering from dysentery he had caught in Martinique, reacted infrequently and with only cautious enthusiasm to Van Gogh's numerous letters. At the time they had agreed to make the exchange of works the previous December, the two artists scarcely knew each other, to judge from a letter Gauguin sent about the arrangements. It began 'Cher Monsieur' (Dear Sir) [576], and continued in a formal, businesslike manner.

Perhaps they got to know each other a little better over the following weeks before Gauguin departed for Brittany in early February 1888. By the time Gauguin sent his next letter to Van Gogh – which had to be forwarded to Arles as the latter had moved south – his tone had warmed. Instead of 'Dear Sir', it began, 'Mon cher Vincent' [581].

Their relationship over the following eight months was entirely carried out by long-distance correspondence. This meant that Gauguin got to know Van Gogh as we do today, through the written word – at his eloquent, impassioned, brilliant best. In person, as Theo acknowledged, Vincent made even the denizens of bohemian Paris, accustomed to eccentric behaviour, so uneasy that he could not persuade models to pose and was forbidden to work in the streets because of constant 'scenes'.[15]

Towards the end of July, Gauguin sent Van Gogh an encouraging letter. He had various ideas for paintings he could do in the south running through his head and would 'very much like it if we were to achieve our aims, that is, my coming to Provence'. He ended: 'Until we're together, an affectionate handshake' [646]. Then, in the last week in August, another heartening letter (now lost) arrived in the post.

These messages raised Vincent's hopes and perhaps melded with another thought. He had an urge to hang his paintings in Arles in a typical Provençal setting. He mentioned this to Theo. 'Here in the south it would do a hell of a lot of good to see paintings on the white walls' [644]. What better way to deck out the Yellow House than with paintings of sunflowers? After all, it was the flower of the south and of the later summer, the bloom that stood for life and love – and the subject of two pictures by Van Gogh which Gauguin already owned.

When he wrote this enthusiastic missive to Theo, on 21 or 22 August, he had already begun work on three sunflower canvases and planned at least one more, which suggests that he had started the project at the beginning of the week. In a letter to Bernard, written about the same time or a day or so earlier, Vincent had described this idea – but implied he had not yet, or only just, begun it. He mentioned he was 'thinking of' decorating his studio with 'half a dozen paintings

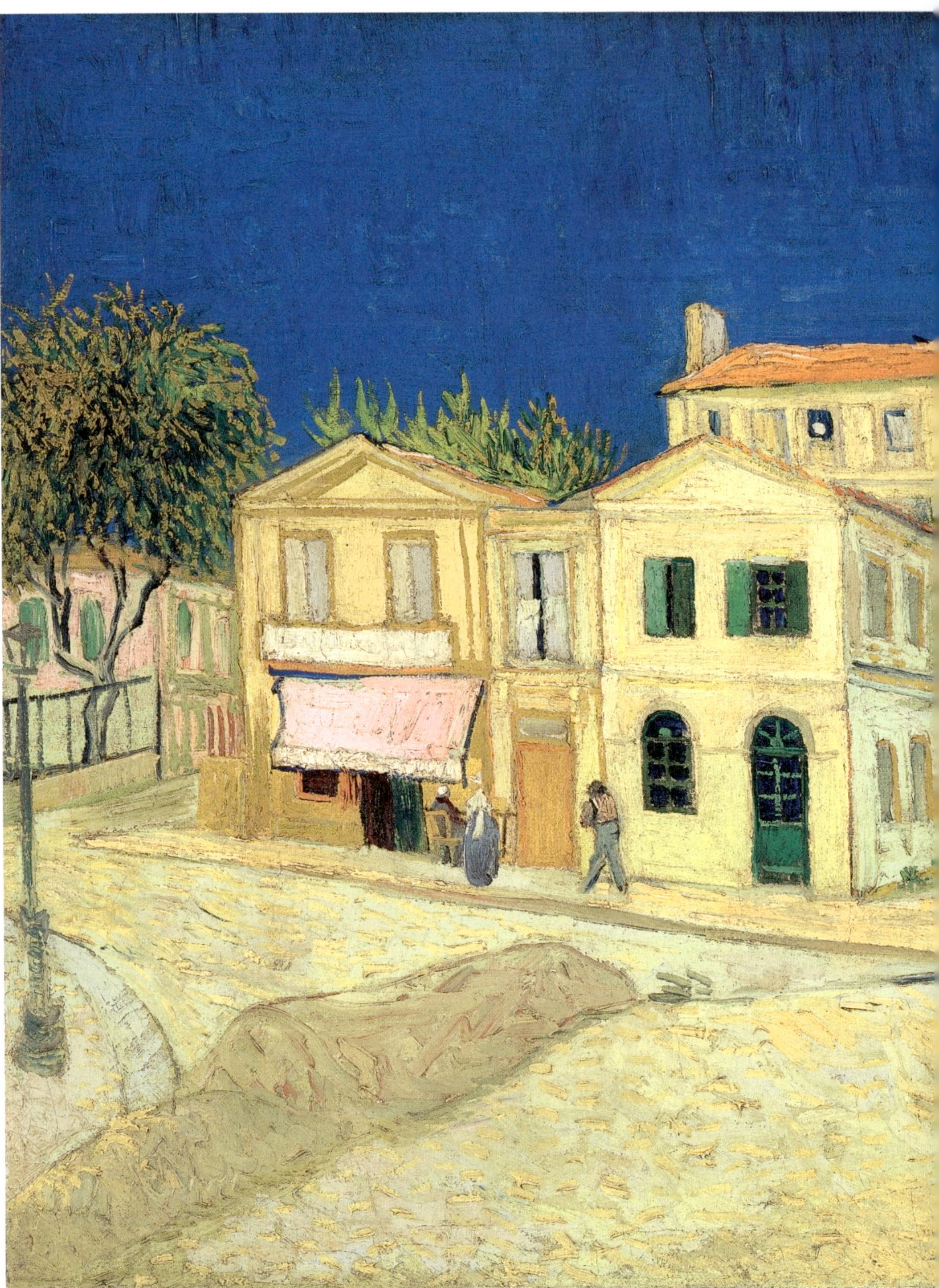

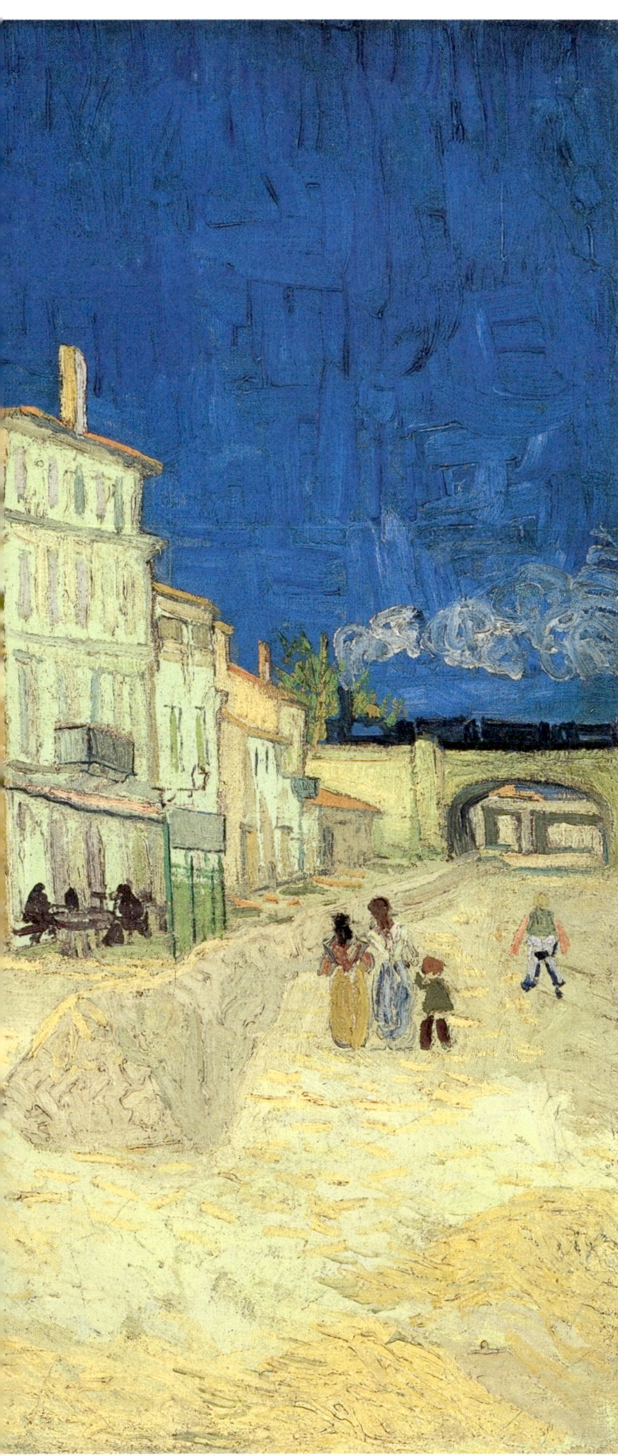

14 *The Yellow House (The Street)*, 1888
Oil on canvas, 72 × 91.5 cm
Van Gogh Museum, Amsterdam
(Vincent van Gogh Foundation)

of *Sunflowers*' [665]. In either case, he was painting this series of pictures at an astonishing rate.

Van Gogh described to Bernard how he imagined these paintings in entirely colouristic terms. In the Yellow House, he explained, there would be 'a decoration in which harsh or broken yellows will burst against various blue backgrounds, from the palest Veronese to royal blue, framed with thin laths painted in orange lead'.

Perhaps only hours later, he listed the first three canvases to Theo. One depicted three 'large flowers in a green vase', with a light blue-green background. The next was also of three flowers which, at the time he wrote, had 'one flower that's gone to seed and lost its petals and a bud' [666]. This was on a royal blue background. These two were on 'no. 25'-sized canvases (81×65 cm, according to the standardised dimensions set in nineteenth-century France). Next, on a still larger no. 30 canvas (92×73 cm), he was painting 'twelve flowers and buds in a yellow vase'. This was again on a light blue background, like the first, but this time the table on which the vase was set was, rather than being brownish, as in the first, or bluish, as in the second, a strong ochre yellow.

Vincent foresaw that he would have to work fast, 'because the flowers wilt quickly and it's a matter of doing the whole thing in one go'. This is confirmation that he was working with real flowers in front of him (perhaps from the nearby bathhouse garden).

The first of the paintings was the most conventional (fig. 15). It depicts three sunflower blooms in an earthenware pot, the upper part of which is covered with an irregular area of green glaze, the remaining portion white. It looks as though it might have been painted from reality. While Provençal pots of this kind could fit three flower heads like this, they are, however, too small and low to contain 12 or 14 tall, heavy sunflowers as shown in the third and fourth canvases; the arrangement would immediately topple over.[16] In another nod to the reality of the scene, Van Gogh owned

15 *Sunflowers*, 1888
Oil on canvas, 73.5×60 cm
Private collection

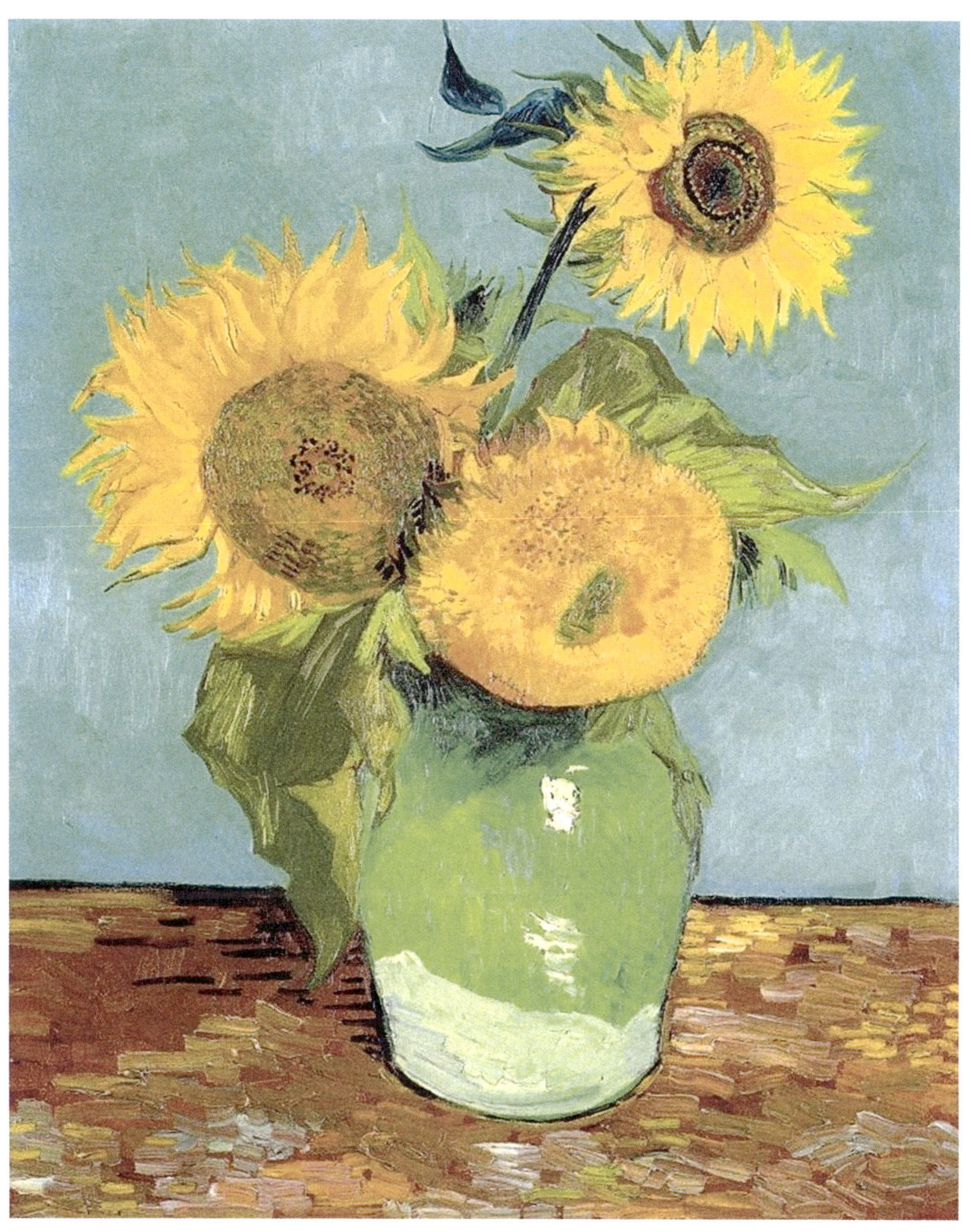

a bare wooden table, just like the surface in the picture (depicted again in a still life the following January).[17]

Up to a point, then, Van Gogh might have been painting more or less what he saw in front of him. However, other elements, even in this first picture, were not derived from observation, but from what he thought – and imagined. Behind the flowers is a light blue-green wall, which harmonises beautifully with the oranges and yellows of the blooms. We know from other pictures and descriptions that the little house at 2 place Lamartine was 'whitewashed inside' (as Vincent informed Willemien) [626]. Therefore, in one important respect he was not transcribing external facts but inventing colour harmonies, much like a composer of music. This was indeed exactly how he described the sunflower decoration to Theo: 'Well, if I carry out this plan there'll be a dozen or so panels. The whole thing will therefore be a symphony in blue and yellow' [666].

Less than six months later, Theo used exactly the same metaphor in a letter in which he was instructing his fiancée Jo on how to appreciate a Gauguin. He took as an example a landscape currently in stock at the gallery where he worked. This picture, Theo began, 'affects me in the same way as a beautiful symphony'.[18] In his eyes, it was an extended exercise in colour harmony. In the centre was a large dead beech tree, 'turned reddish-orange', around which 'the deep bluish and violet shadows of the full trees' stood out 'against the orange, like two melodies in counter-point'. These were 'echoed in unusual shades of green & fade in parts into the blue of the sky above', while a white cloud, some peasants dressed in blue and a verdant meadow added subsidiary themes, 'like little melodies', in contrast to the grand chromatic drama of red-orange and blue-violet. This was how the brothers Van Gogh (and Gauguin) thought about colour.

Gauguin had written to Vincent in July, replying to a now-lost letter: 'I entirely agree with you on the slight importance that accuracy contributes to art' [646]. It was

16 *Sunflowers*, 1888
Oil on canvas, 98×69 cm
Lost during the Second World War. Recreation made in 2017 by Factum Arte for 'Mystery of the Lost Paintings' (Sky Arts, 2018) in collaboration with Ballandi Arts.

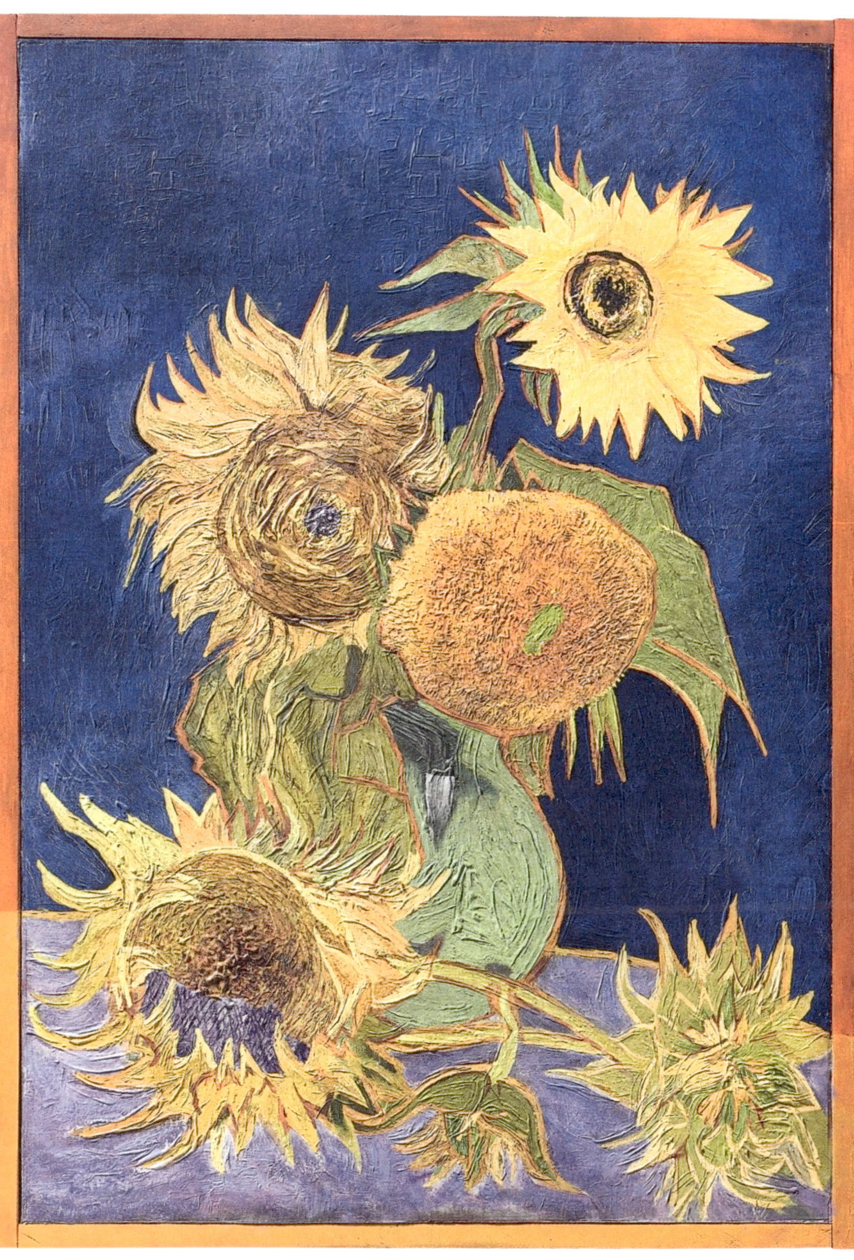

one of Gauguin's tenets that 'art is an abstraction'. A detail such as a wall being white was no reason not to paint it blue.

This process went much further in the second picture. Although this work was destroyed by bombing in Japan during the Second World War, it is fortunately known from a colour photograph (fig. 16).[19] This reveals that the basic set-up for this painting was almost exactly the same as that for the first – but everything else about it had changed.

The light blue wall has been transformed into a rich ultramarine, recalling the deep blue with which Van Gogh painted the midsummer Mediterranean sky. The tabletop has turned light violet and the pot is now a solid, flat green, unrelieved by shadows or highlights but given body by a patterning of thick brush marks. The most striking alteration, however, is the way that most, though not quite all, of the objects in the picture are surrounded by an emphatic outline – red around the green leaves, pot and vase, but light yellow or orange around the leaves, stalks and blooms that lie on the violet tabletop.

These outlines are in hues calculated to contrast and complement the ground on which they were painted – red against the dark blue, yellow or orange against the light purple of the table. This must be the effect Van Gogh had in mind when he described his project for a decoration of sunflowers to Bernard as being like that of the '*stained-glass windows* of a Gothic church' [665]. To Theo, he described this contour as a 'halo', explaining: 'that's to say, each object is surrounded by a line of the colour complementary to the background against which it stands out' [668].

ALL IN YELLOW, ALL IN ORANGE, ALL IN SULPHUR[20]

Vincent had given Theo another hint of what he was thinking in his letter of 21 or 22 August: 'I'm beginning more and more to look for a simple technique that perhaps isn't Impressionist. I'd like to paint in such a way that if it comes to it, everyone who has eyes could understand it' [666].

What he meant was evident in the third sunflower picture of that month (fig. 4). This is as extraordinary for its texture as for its colour. The ground behind the flowers is an almost unchanging light greenish blue. But the brushstrokes that make it up form a visible pattern of horizontal and vertical strokes like basket weave. This is continued in the butter-coloured surface of the table below, while the pot is rendered with a more irregular mixture of upright and cross-strokes suggesting its rotundity, plus a squiggle of white for the highlight.

The flowers are almost literally modelled. As far as possible, Van Gogh made each petal and leaf from a single vehement stroke, often reinforced by an equally bold outline drawn in paint of a darker tone. The florets in the centre are mimicked by a dense mass of paint suggesting their bristling density.

While painting this canvas and the fourth, culminating sunflower canvas of this series (fig. 1), Vincent was thinking about the physical texture of the materials he was using. To Theo he mused about the possibility of persuading Guillaume Charles Tasset, who ran the artists' supplies shop they used, to produce paints that were less finely ground. He thought this change in the process would produce a less oily result, so the resulting paint surface would be less shiny, more matt in effect. Academic artists – such as the star of the annual exhibition at the Paris Salon, Jean-Léon Gérôme – liked their paints as smooth-flowing and oily as possible, aiding the '*trompe-l'oeil* photographic' look of their works. 'We', Vincent went on, meaning 'he', 'on the contrary, don't strongly object to the canvas having a rough look' [668].

One of his inspirations was the rebellious Edouard Manet. 'Do you remember', he asked Theo in the same letter, 'that one day at the Hôtel Drouot we saw a quite extraordinary Manet, some large pink peonies and their green leaves on a light background?' They had seen this work at a sale on 5 June 1886, not long after Vincent had arrived in Paris (fig. 17). Evidently it had lodged in his mind.

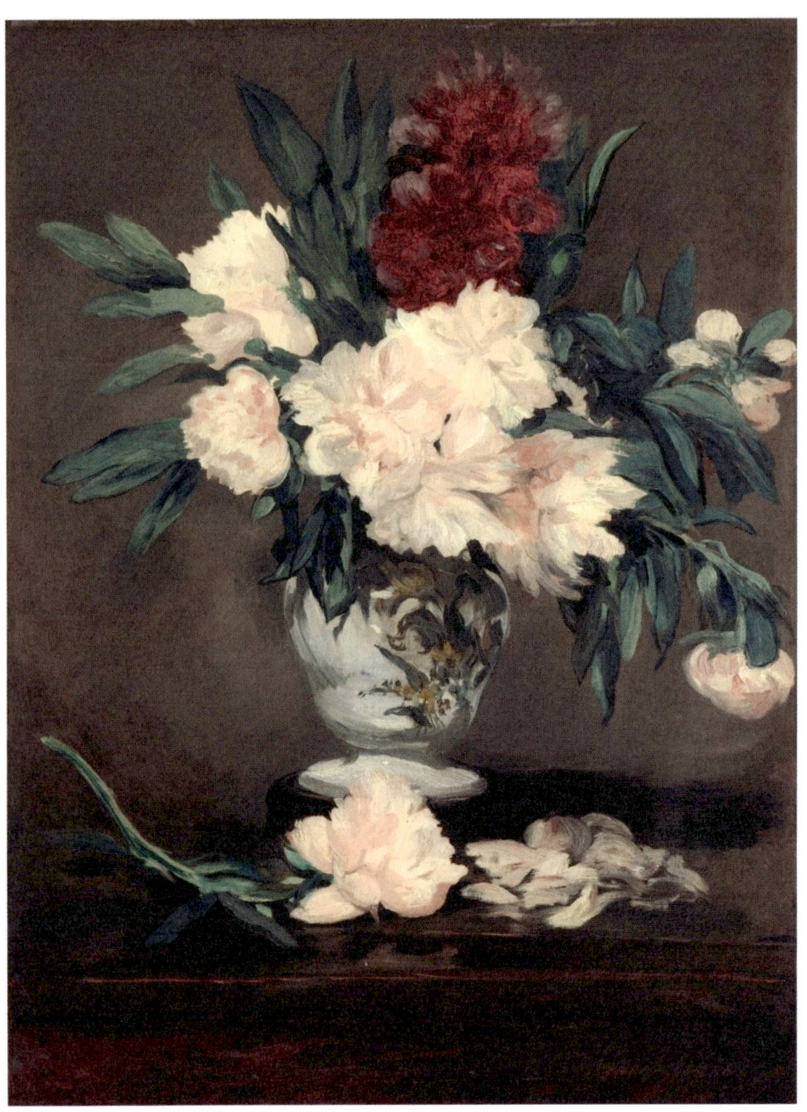

17 Edouard Manet (1832–1883)
Vase of Peonies on a Pedestal, 1864
Oil on canvas, 93.3×70 cm
Musée d'Orsay, Paris

18 Adolphe Monticelli (1824–1886)
Vase of Flowers, about 1875
Oil on panel, 51×39 cm
Van Gogh Museum, Amsterdam
(Vincent van Gogh Foundation)

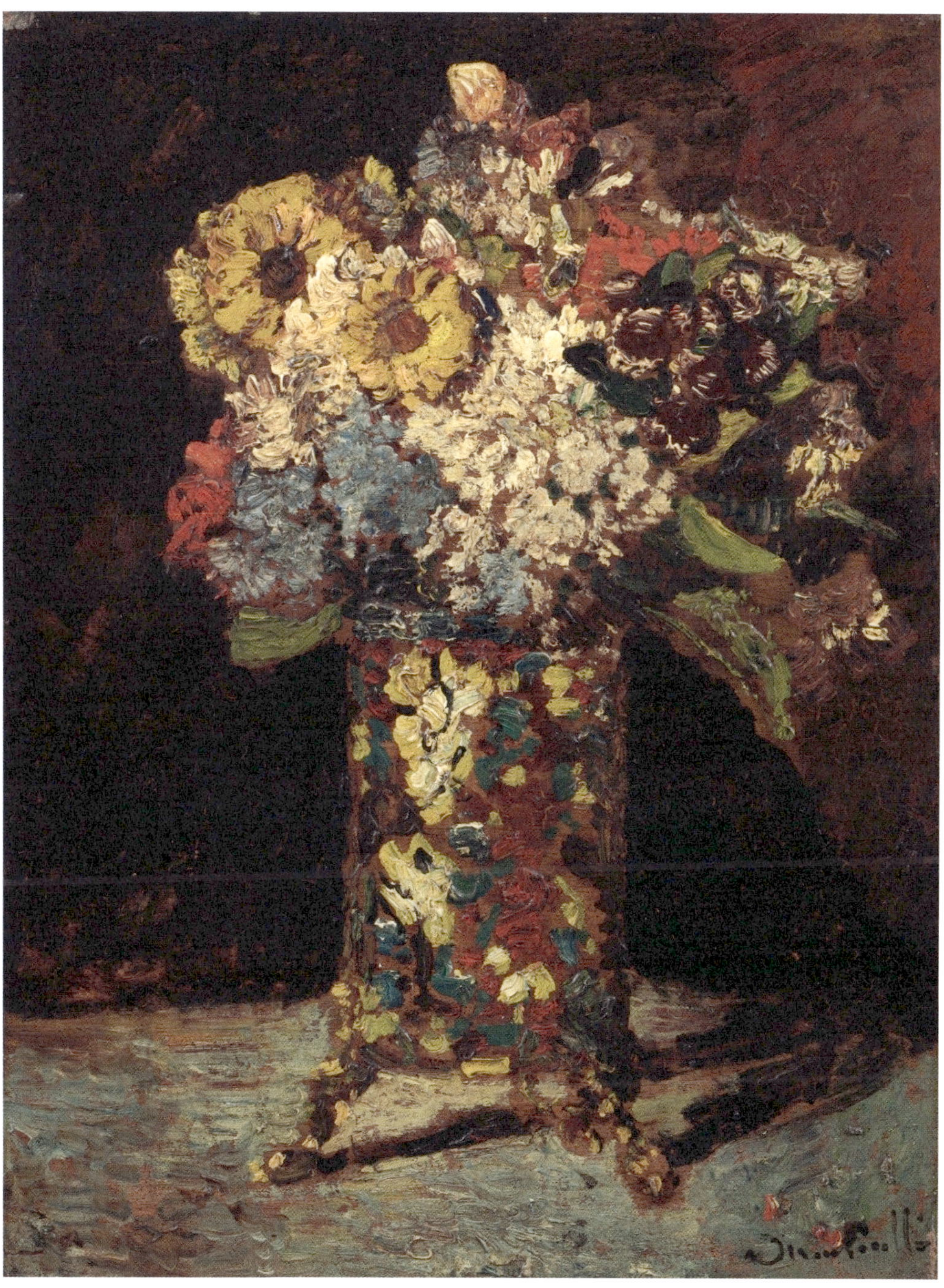

Part of the reason for this was the way it was executed: 'As much in harmony and as much a *flower* as anything you like, and yet painted in solid, thick impasto.' Among nineteenth-century French painters Manet was renowned (as he still is) as a great exponent of the brushstroke. This was a manner of working that Van Gogh greatly admired – and in which he excelled. He compared his own 'decoration' almost to 'barbotine' [694] – that is, pottery decorated with liquid clay or slip.

The other reason why this Manet had so struck Van Gogh was perhaps that it was verging on monochrome. It depicts mainly white flowers in a bluish-white vase against a whitish-grey background. This effect was far more muted than that of the final, extraordinary sunflower painting Van Gogh painted that August. But the principle was similar. After he finally arrived in Arles, late in October, Gauguin probably heard a great deal about Manet and those flowers. Vincent's conversation was repetitive and it is likely that Gauguin was told in person a good deal of what was written to others on paper.[21]

There was another master of the brushstroke whom Van Gogh revered, but about whom Gauguin disagreed. While Manet could evoke an object such as a petal with a single flourish in such a way that the paint just seemed to turn into the plant, the impasto of the Marseillaise artist Adolphe Monticelli was much more extreme, piled up and impacted like putty on the canvas (fig. 18). Van Gogh loved this effect; Gauguin did not. Later in the autumn he confided disapprovingly to a friend that Van Gogh 'has an eye for blobs of impasto in the manner of Monticelli, whereas I detest all that messing about with brushwork and that kind of thing'.[22]

By the time Vincent wrote to Theo again towards the end of the week, he had added another picture to the sunflower scheme that was yet more daring than what he had described to Bernard. 'I'm now on the fourth painting of sunflowers. This fourth one is a bouquet of 14 flowers and is on a yellow background' [668]. This is the picture now in the National Gallery (fig. 1).

Like two of the others, the painting seems to have grown after he first described it. The 3 sunflowers on royal blue became 6, the one of 12 expanded to 14, and this last picture of 14 extruded one light green, scarcely opened bud on a drooping stem to become a depiction of 15 blooms. No doubt Van Gogh made these additions to balance the compositions – and also the whole ensemble. Without that final bud, the yellow-on-yellow work would have looked lopsided.

In his letter to Bernard, he had speculated that if he completed his plan, there would be 'half a dozen' sunflower paintings on the walls of his studio [665]. In practice, however, he stopped after four, the reason perhaps being that he had completed the trajectory – and made one of the most startling breakthroughs in the history of Western painting. This was because the work was both vibrant in hue and effectively monochrome. Or – as Gauguin claimed a (probably imaginary) Italian artist reacted to a similar Van Gogh painting – 'Merde! merde! Everything is yellow! I don't know what painting is any longer!'[23]

Van Gogh's previous paintings (and Gauguin's too) had been based on the theory of colour, by which red, yellow and blue were 'primary'. These could be mixed to produce a 'secondary' colour (blue + yellow = green). Each primary colour had a 'complementary' secondary. Thus the complement of red was green, of blue it was orange, and of yellow, purple. In a later version, this was amended slightly so that the complement of blue was yellow. But Van Gogh also combined yellows and oranges in these pictures. And in the fourth and final one, he burst through the system altogether into brand-new territory.

What he was doing was equivalent to abandoning the conventional structure in music. Instead of creating a balance of complementary and more closely related colours, as Gauguin had done in the landscape that Theo described to Jo, Vincent had broken through into a world in which

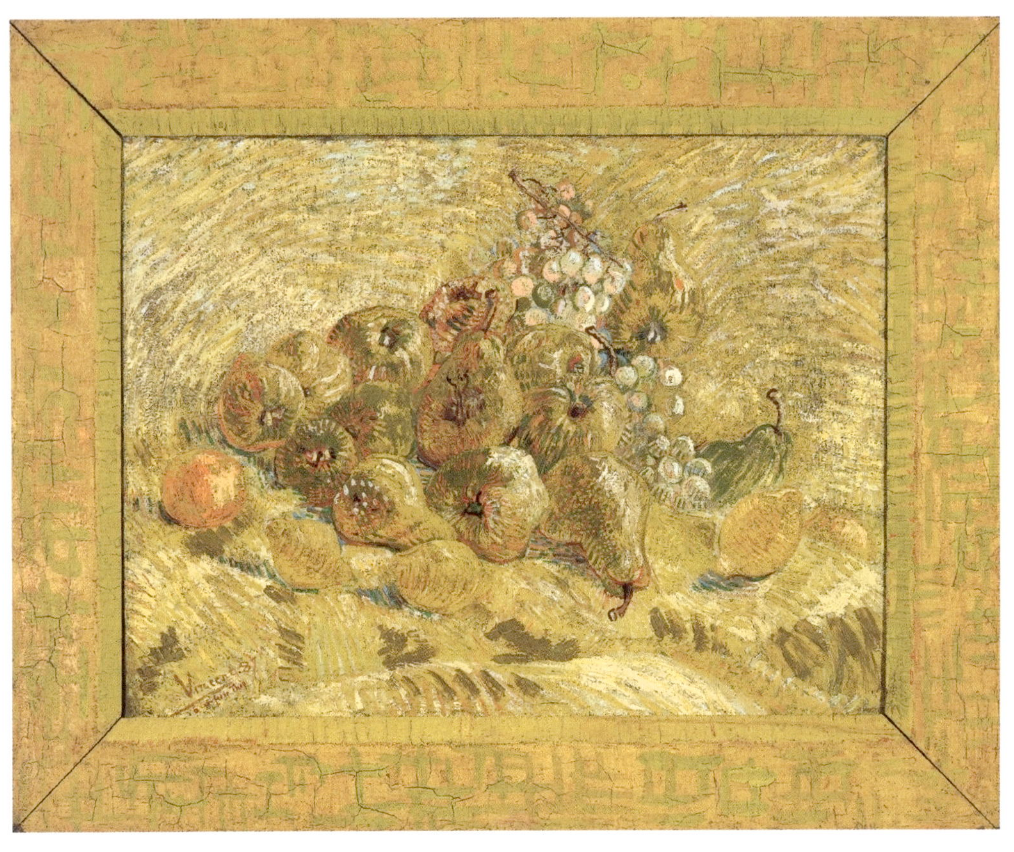

19 *Quinces, Lemons, Pears and Grapes*, 1887
Oil on canvas, 48.9×65.5 cm
Van Gogh Museum, Amsterdam (Vincent van Gogh Foundation)

20 *Sunflowers*, 1889
Oil on canvas, 95×73 cm
Van Gogh Museum, Amsterdam (Vincent van Gogh Foundation)

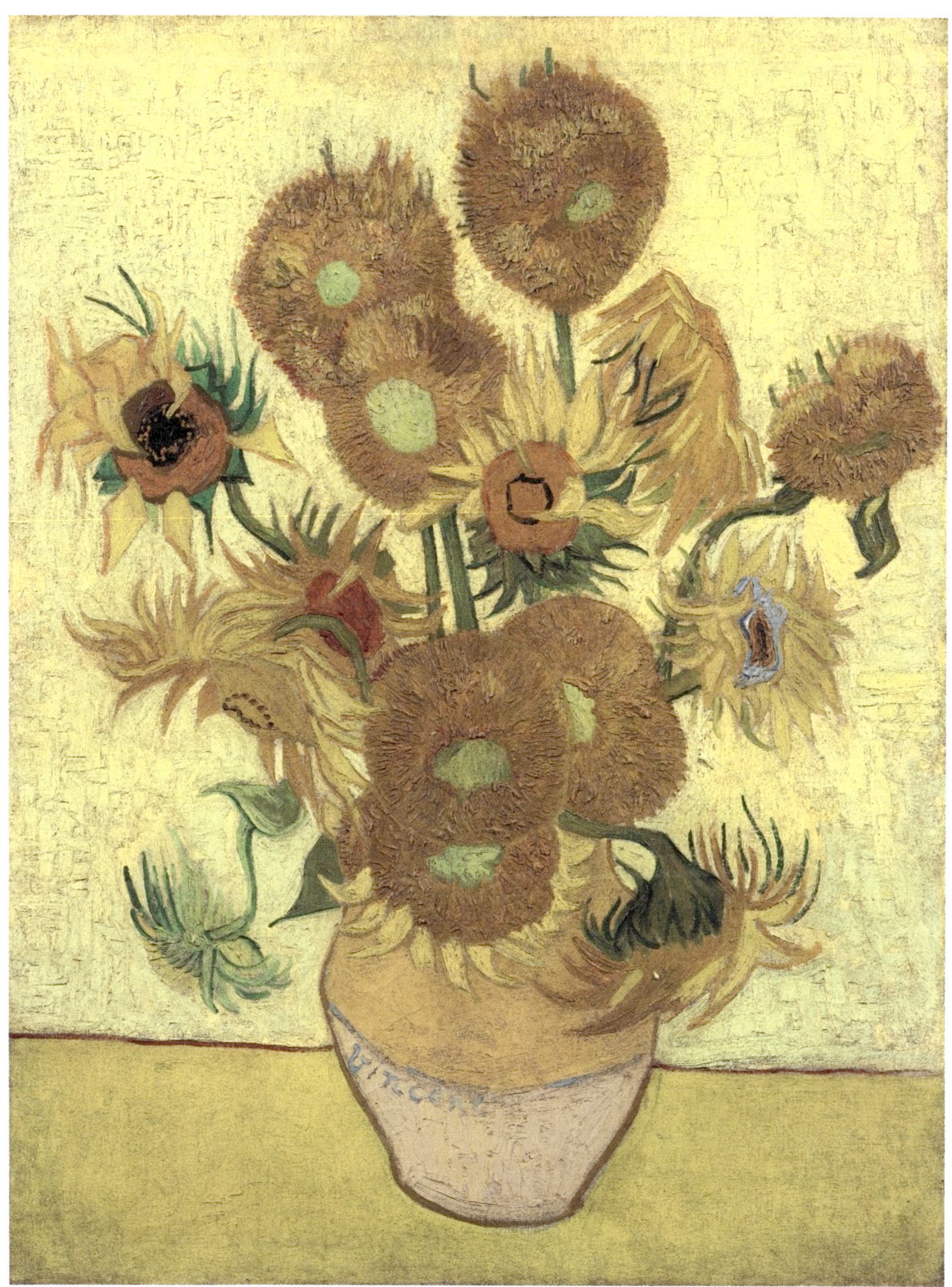

almost everything was yellow (or orange, which was virtually the same thing). What Van Gogh had produced in this fourth picture was more like a single, overpowering chord.

Although there are touches of other colours – a few green stalks and leaves, the blue signature and dividing line between tabletop and wall – the picture is almost entirely executed in shades and tones of yellow: ochres, lemons, orange tints, cream tinged with butter. This was not, as Vincent pointed out to Theo, the first such painting he had made. A still life of quinces, lemons, pears and grapes he had painted in early autumn 1887 was the same in this respect – he even made a yellow frame for it, which still survives (fig. 19). But this yellow-on-yellow sunflowers, he realised, had much more impact. This he felt, correctly, was partly because it was 'much bigger', but also because it was painted with 'more simplicity'. And by that Vincent meant that it was executed entirely in clear, legible brushstrokes of 'solid, thick impasto'. The combination of condensed simplicity, clarity and insistent, blazing colour gave the image a vehement power. It was charged with Van Gogh's passion and retained some of the poignancy of the sunflower – which, like the artist, blooms so spectacularly, then wilts and dies.

In Van Gogh's imagination the sunflowers burnt like solar discs. While explaining the project to Theo, he wrote of 'décorations de soleils', decorations of *suns* rather than sunflowers, 'tournesols' – a revealing slip [668]. Vincent's favourite metaphor for the sun of Provence was 'sulphur', a chemical element that burns yellow. 'There's sulphur everywhere where the sun beats down' [610]. He described how 'a great sun like sulphur' shone on the women of Arles in their vividly coloured clothes, out of a 'vast blue sky' [653].

When newly completed, this and the other sunflower pictures would also have been brighter than they now appear. However, as Van Gogh sadly noted the following April, paintings often 'fade like flowers' [765]. This fate has befallen his own pictures over time – and detailed research has revealed just how they have been affected. The geranium lake reds and yellow ochres he used tend, respectively, to darken and grow fainter over time. As a result of such changes, 'the yellow ball-shaped blooms in the middle were originally far more orange and have browned. His signature and the centre of a flower were purple and have turned light blue.'[24] Although this description is of a later replica Van Gogh made (fig. 20), the same would be true of the National Gallery picture. We must imagine just how vivid these works once were – and how much of a surprise (shock, even) Gauguin must have had when he first encountered them on his bedroom wall.

SUNFLOWERS STUFFED INTO THIS TINY LITTLE BOUDOIR[25]

In early September, Van Gogh threw himself into an even more ambitious project. Now it seemed likely Gauguin would soon be travelling south to join him, Van Gogh decided to prepare the Yellow House as a dwelling where they both could live. From his initial decorative scheme of sunflower paintings, this grew into something more like an exhibition – almost a manifesto – summarising everything he had seen, felt and achieved in this place. Many of the paintings he included in this 'decoration' depicted the house itself, including his bedroom (fig. 21), and its environs. But the sunflowers retained a place of honour in the guest bedroom next door, the 'prettiest room', which would be Gauguin's (or Theo's, if he came to stay):

> Opening the window in the morning, you see the greenery in the gardens and the rising sun and the entrance of the town. But you'll see these big paintings of bouquets of 12, 14 sunflowers stuffed into this tiny little boudoir with a pretty bed and everything else elegant. [677]

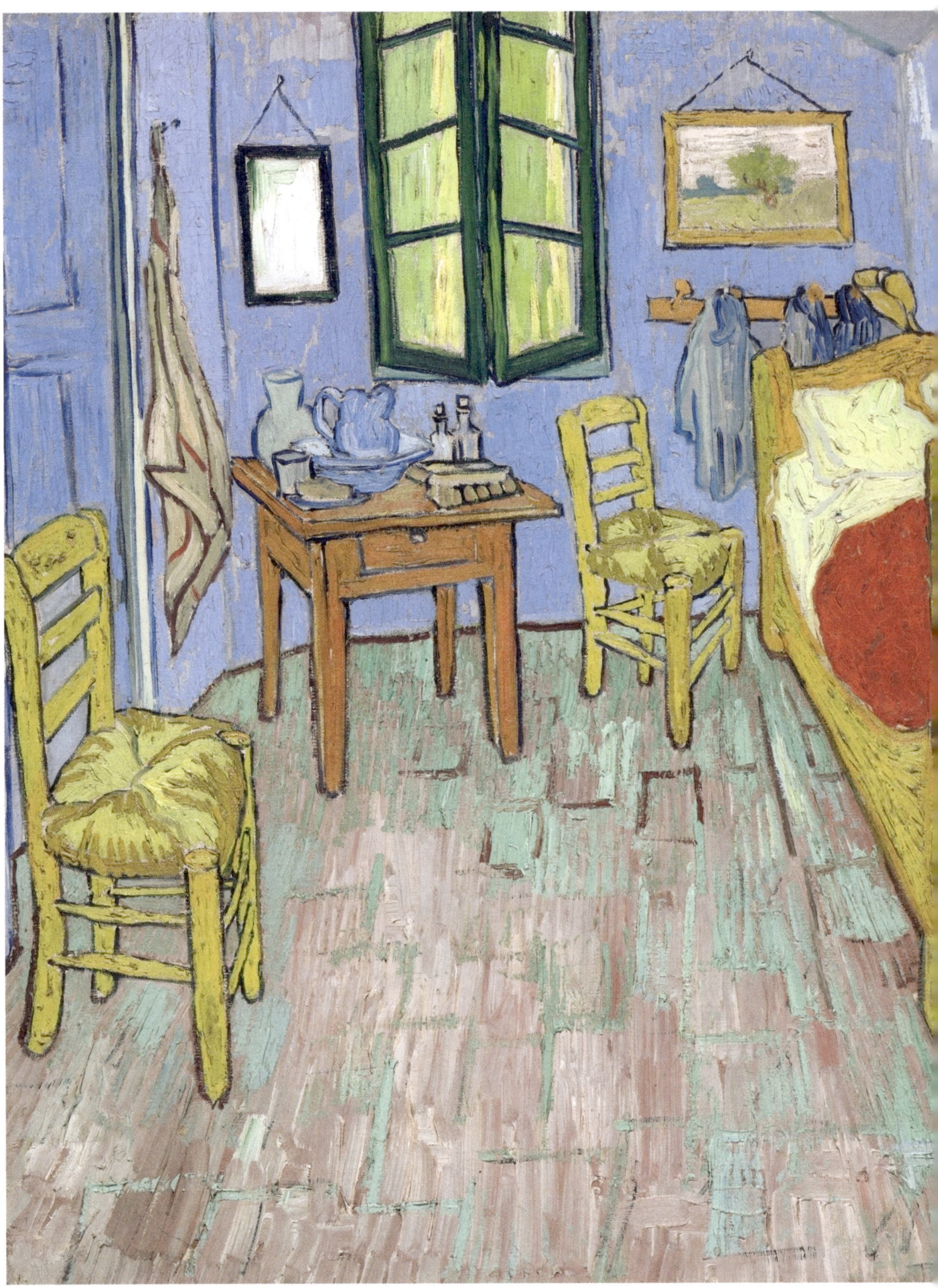

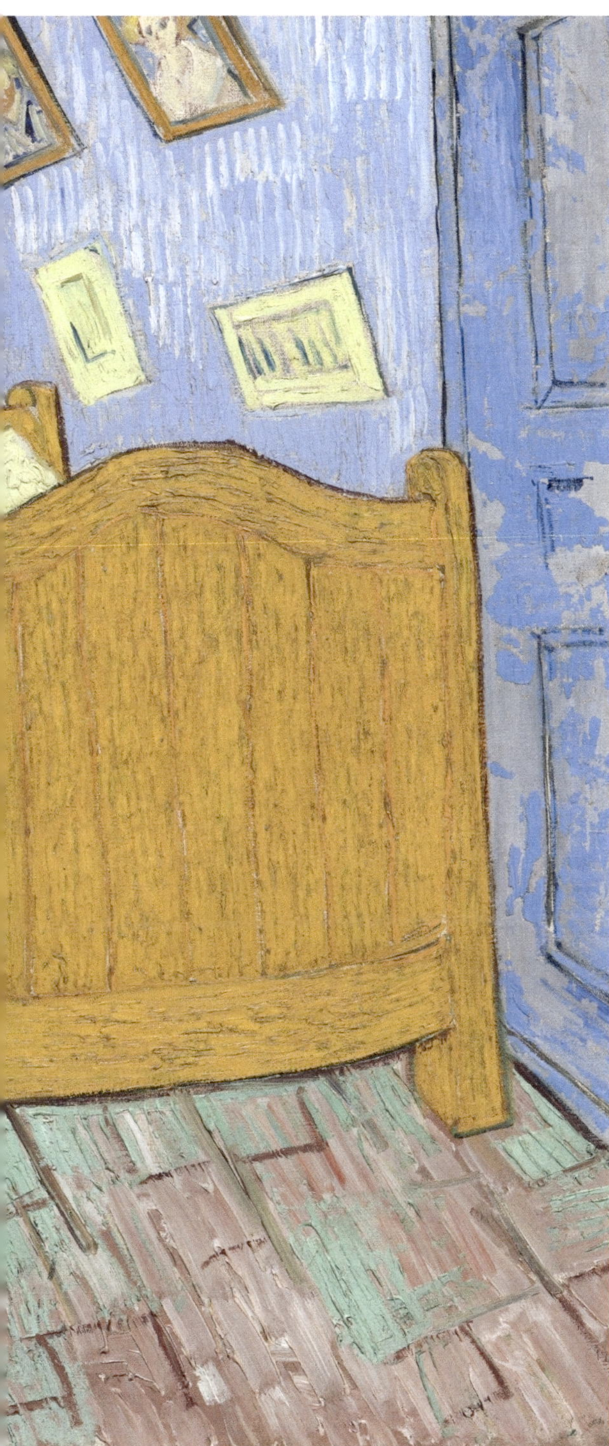

21 *The Bedroom*, 1889
Oil on canvas, 73.6×92.3 cm
The Art Institute of Chicago.
Helen Birch Bartlett Memorial
Collection

This effect, Vincent predicted with satisfaction, would not be 'commonplace'. The power of such paintings in a confined space must have been staggering (the two sunflower pictures were accompanied by three paintings of the little municipal park outside the window). Gauguin did not record his first reaction, when he finally stepped through the door on 23 October. But Vincent mentioned that 'Gauguin himself above all liked the sunflowers later, when he had seen them for a long time' [776]. It sounds as if, even though he was one of the most avant-garde artists in Europe, it took him time to get used to these extraordinary works.

Gauguin's complimentary remarks about the *Sunflowers* – that they were better than Monet – were made in the second half of November when he had been living alongside them for almost a month. Shortly afterwards, he painted Van Gogh at work on a canvas of sunflowers (fig. 2). It may be, although this dating has been disputed, that at this point Van Gogh made a replica of the 15 yellow-on-yellow sunflowers painting (fig. 22). On the same occasion, perhaps at Gauguin's instigation, he used the coarse jute canvas which Gauguin had bought, producing an even more heavily textured effect.[26]

The following January, after Van Gogh had suffered his horrifying mental crisis and severed most of his left ear just before Christmas, Gauguin, who had fled Arles in panic, paid the *Sunflowers* an even greater compliment. He asked Vincent to give them to him.

At first, Van Gogh – only partially recovered from his breakdown and resentful about Gauguin's desertion – was put out by this: 'I find it quite odd that he's claiming a painting of sunflowers from me, offering me in exchange I suppose, or as a gift, a few studies that he left here' [736]. A few days later, on 21 January, he wrote in a more positive mood: 'You talk to me in your letter about a canvas of mine, the sunflowers with a yellow background – to say that it would give you some pleasure to receive it' [739]. Despite everything, he was flattered by Gauguin's interest in this

22 *Sunflowers*, 1888
Oil on canvas, 100.5×76.5 cm
Sompo Museum of Art, Tokyo

Overleaf:
23 *La Berceuse (The Lullaby)*, 1889
Oil on canvas, 92.7×72.7 cm
Museum of Fine Arts, Boston. Bequest of John T. Spaulding

24 *Sunflowers*, 1889
Oil on canvas, 92.4×71.1 cm
Philadelphia Museum of Art, Pennsylvania
The Mr and Mrs Carroll S. Tyson, Jr, Collection, 1963

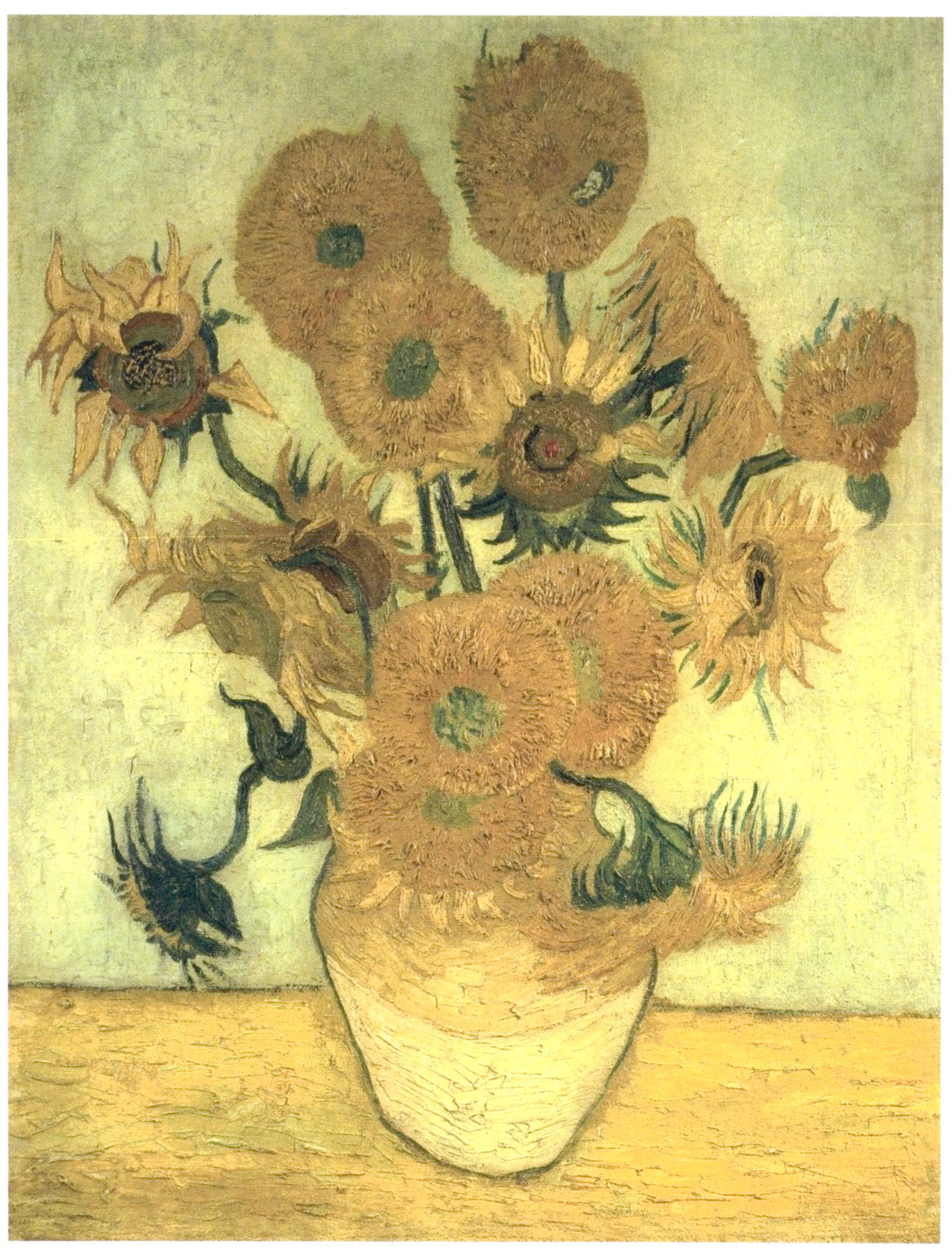

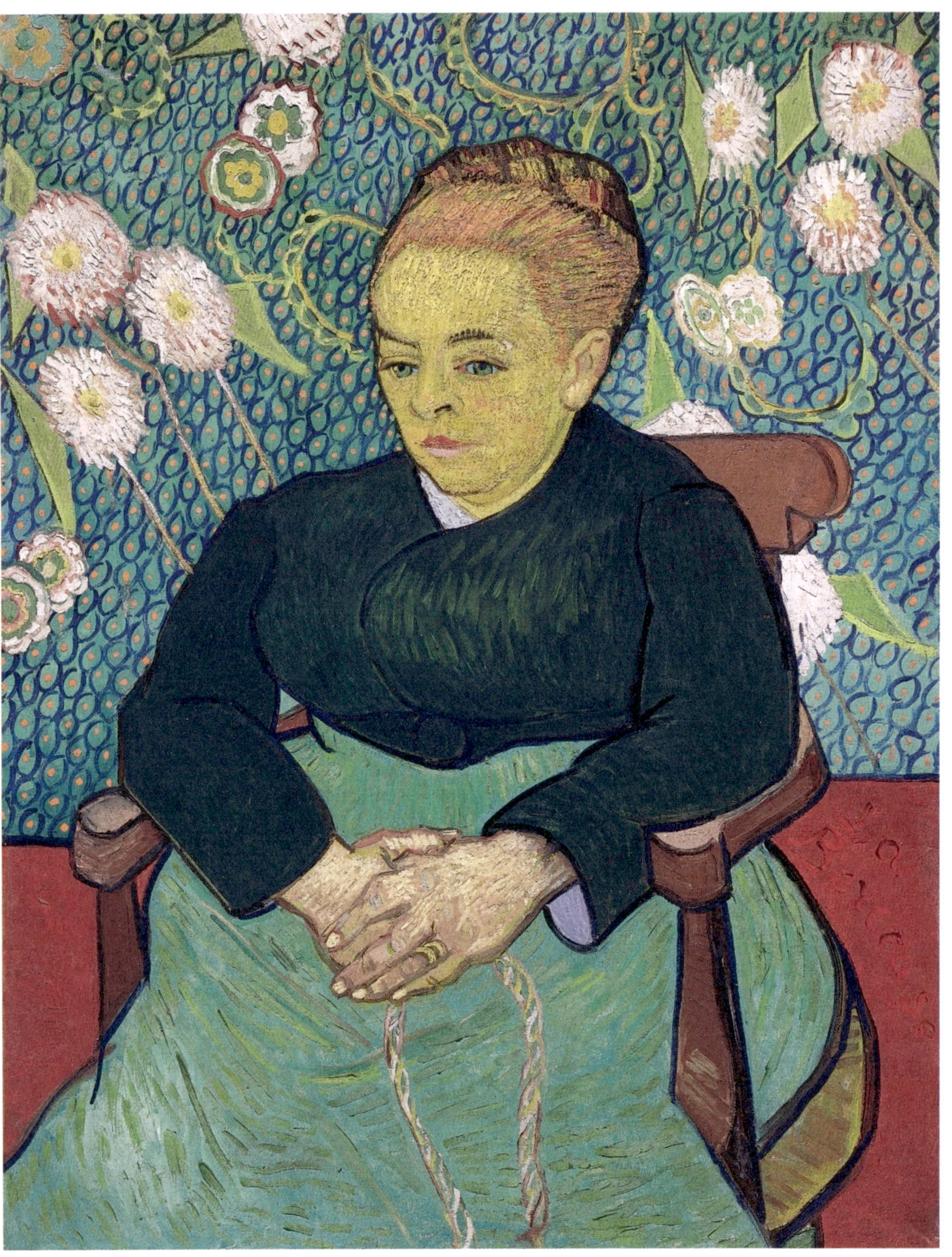

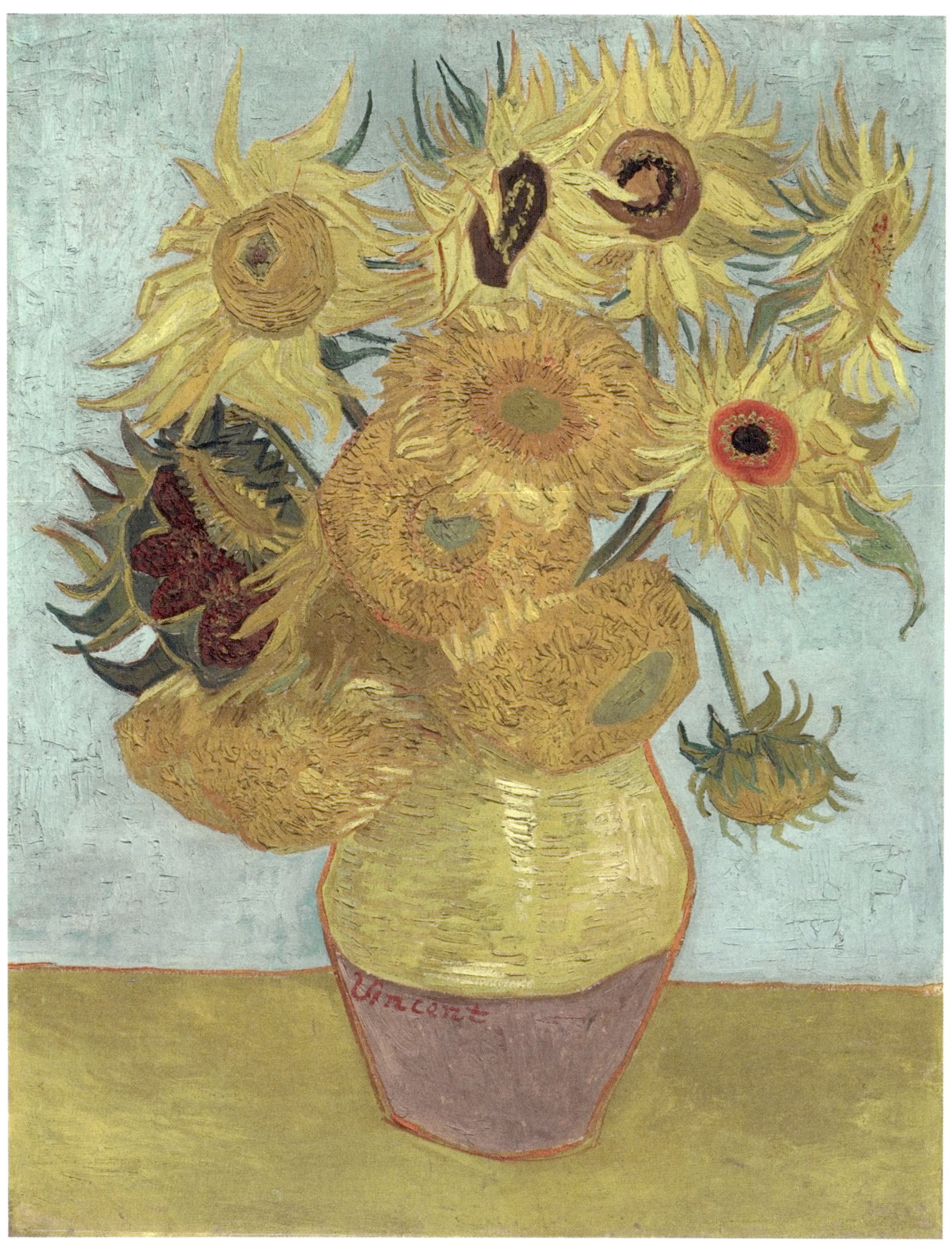
Vincent

picture. 'I don't think that you've made a bad choice,' he conceded. He went on to name two celebrated flower-painting specialists of the day, Georges Jeannin and Ernest Quost – where 'Jeannin has the peony, Quost the hollyhock, I indeed, before others, have taken the sunflower': but he, Van Gogh, was the finest exponent of the sunflower.

This is sometimes translated as 'the sunflowers are mine' – one of the most confidently self-assertive statements about his work that Van Gogh ever made. It was a measure of how pleased he was with the yellow-on-yellow composition. As far as Gauguin's request was concerned, he unbent somewhat. Van Gogh wanted to hold on to the originals, but he was prepared to make copies, 'so that you could have your own all the same'.

He set about doing this, making two 'absolutely equivalent and identical repetitions' [743] of the paintings in Gauguin's bedroom within a week. These are the works now in the Van Gogh Museum (fig. 20) and the Philadelphia Museum of Art (fig. 24). By the French word he used to describe them, *répétition*, Van Gogh perhaps meant that he was not so much copying as *remaking* these pictures. Crucially, he did not have a real bouquet set up in front of his easel, but another picture. As he worked, he made a series of small changes, for example, altering the colours of various painted outlines or 'haloes'.

As it turned out, Gauguin did not get any of the copies. While Van Gogh was making these repetitions, he was also putting the finishing touches to a portrait of Augustine Roulin, the wife of his friend the postal supervisor Joseph Roulin, rocking the cradle of their baby daughter, Marcelle (known as *La Berceuse*, 'the cradle-rocker', or 'lullaby') (fig. 23). Marcelle was born at the end of July, just before Van Gogh conceived the idea of painting sunflowers. Van Gogh had known the combination of flowers, baby and cradle years before in The Hague. In early autumn 1882 he had painted 'a study of a courtyard with a bleaching ground and sunflowers' (now lost) [266]. This was when he was living with a sex

25 *Mother with Child*, 1882
Pencil and oils on watercolour paper, 41 × 24.6 cm
Kröller-Müller Museum, Otterlo

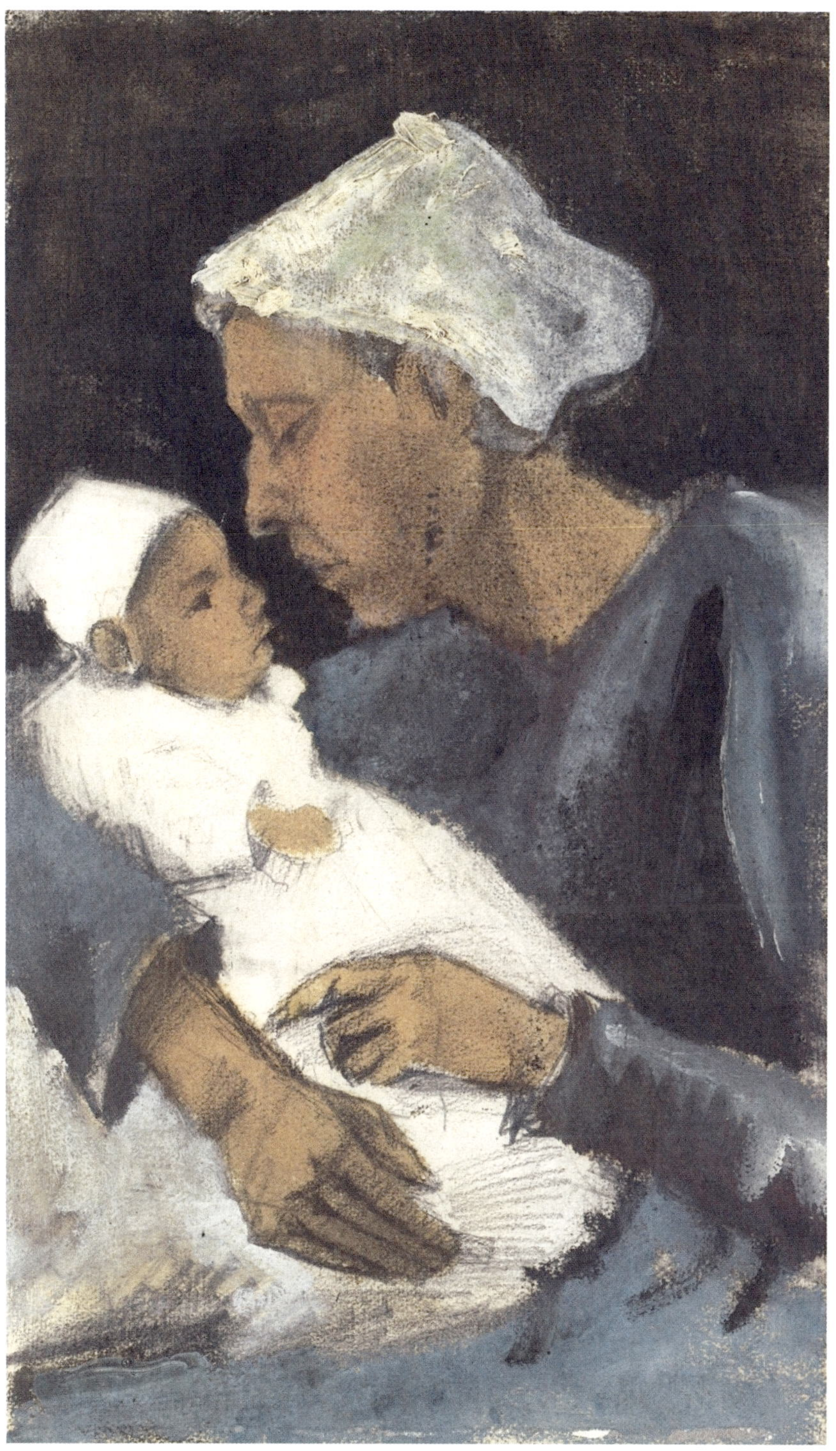

worker, Clasina Maria (Sien) Hoornik, and her children. Sien was pregnant when they met (not by Van Gogh) and gave birth in June to a baby boy, Willem (fig. 25). The presence of new life in his studio gave joy to Van Gogh, who fetched his cradle from a junk shop on his shoulders. For him, that child 'was a light in the house through the whole dark winter' [307]. The sunflowers also stood for life and light. Vincent explained to Willemien that his paintings were 'almost a cry of anguish while symbolising gratitude in the rustic sunflower' [856]. They flared with beauty and vitality, gave pleasure to the eye, then – as he noted – quickly wilted.

Finishing *La Berceuse* gave Vincent the idea of combining the cradle-rocking portrait with the sunflowers. 'I can imagine these canvases precisely between those of the sunflowers – which thus form standard lamps or candelabra at the sides' [743] (fig. 26). He considered multiple arrangements: two sets of three canvases, since he also made copies of *La Berceuse*, even seven or nine pictures lined up together. The only person to see such an exhibition, one of the most extraordinary of its era, was Joseph Roulin, and what he made of it is not recorded.

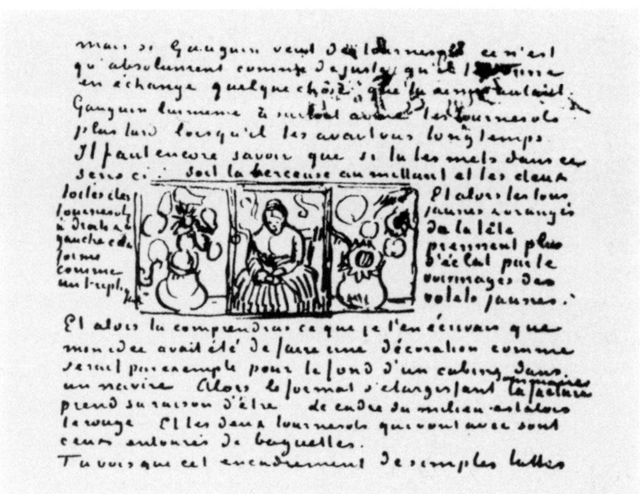

26 Sketch, triptych with *La Berceuse* and two versions of *Sunflowers* in a letter from Vincent to Theo van Gogh, on or about 23 May 1889
Present whereabouts unknown

BRIMMING WITH SUN IN A POT[27]

The *Sunflowers'* time was yet to come. If it took Gauguin a month to get used to them, the rest of the world required years. Van Gogh selected the original yellow-on-yellow canvas to be included with a small group of his paintings in an exhibition in Brussels in January 1890. This was the most significant display of his work shown in his lifetime.

Before the opening, the Belgian artist Henry de Groux threatened to withdraw his own pictures as he did not wish 'to find himself in the same room as the laughable pot of sunflowers by Mr Vincent'. He called Van Gogh, who was then in a psychiatric hospital at Saint-Rémy-de-Provence, 'an ignoramus and a charlatan', at which point Van Gogh's friend Toulouse-Lautrec challenged him to a duel. Bloodshed was averted with difficulty.[28]

When the epoch-making exhibition *Manet and the Post-Impressionists* opened in London in November 1910, it contained 22 Van Goghs, among them two of the yellow-on-yellow *Sunflowers* (one of them probably the original). This was the first real exposure of the British public to modern art, with works by Paul Cezanne, Gauguin, Pablo Picasso, Henri Matisse and others also on view. There followed a predictable explosion of philistinism. But the *Sunflowers* made a deep impact on some visitors. In Britain, perhaps because the public had been made sunflower-conscious by the Pre-Raphaelites and Aesthetes, these Van Goghs became emblematic of the new art of the twentieth century.

The New Zealand writer Katherine Mansfield described seeing a picture of 'yellow flowers – brimming with sun in a pot'. Those blooms 'lived with me afterwards', she went on: 'I can *smell* them as I write.'[29] Mansfield's sensibility was more powerful than her botanical accuracy (sunflowers do not really have a scent), but she was not alone in her reaction.

In 1923, Harold 'Jim' Ede, a youthful curator at the National Gallery, Millbank – subsequently renamed the Tate Gallery – travelled to Amsterdam to see the pictures in Jo van

Gogh-Bonger's apartment. She had inherited almost all of Vincent's work when Theo died in 1891, and over 30 years later still owned the vast bulk of it. Ede saw many masterpieces, and even toyed with the idea of buying a still life, *Parisian Novels*, from his meagre salary and presenting it to the nation. But, as he wrote to Jo from his hotel, 'what touches me most directly are the golden sunflowers'. He asked if she might sell the picture, 'to be exhibited at the fountainhead of England's art'.[30]

She refused. But in early 1924, exactly 100 years since the foundation of the National Gallery, after further pleas and an internal struggle lasting two days, Jo unexpectedly changed her mind. Even more surprisingly, she parted with the original, not with Vincent's copy, which remained in the family collection and is now in the Van Gogh Museum (fig. 20). Her reason for changing her mind is clear from her reply; she knew this was what Vincent himself would have wanted. London was a city in which he had lived for formative years in his youth, and he knew the galleries well (he recommended Theo look out for particular works by John Constable and Meindert Hobbema in the National Gallery). As Jo wrote, 'no picture would represent Vincent in your famous Gallery in a more worthy manner than the "Sunflowers", and that he ... would have liked it to be there'.[31]

At this stage, a little more than three decades after his early death, in conservative London Van Gogh still seemed like a contemporary – and a wild, experimental and sometimes disturbing one at that. Charles Aitken, the director of the National Gallery on Millbank (and Ede's boss), had already decided against the purchase of one Van Gogh that year. But a trust generously set up by the textile tycoon Samuel Courtauld to buy Impressionist and Post-Impressionist works for the British nation had acquired three – although the trustees had doubts over a portrait of Vincent's friend Joseph Roulin from early 1889. Admittedly this is one of his more startlingly stylised works; one trustee (perhaps Aitken) thought Roulin's beard looked 'too funny'.[32]

27 *Van Gogh's Chair*, 1888
Oil on canvas, 91.8 × 73 cm
The National Gallery, London

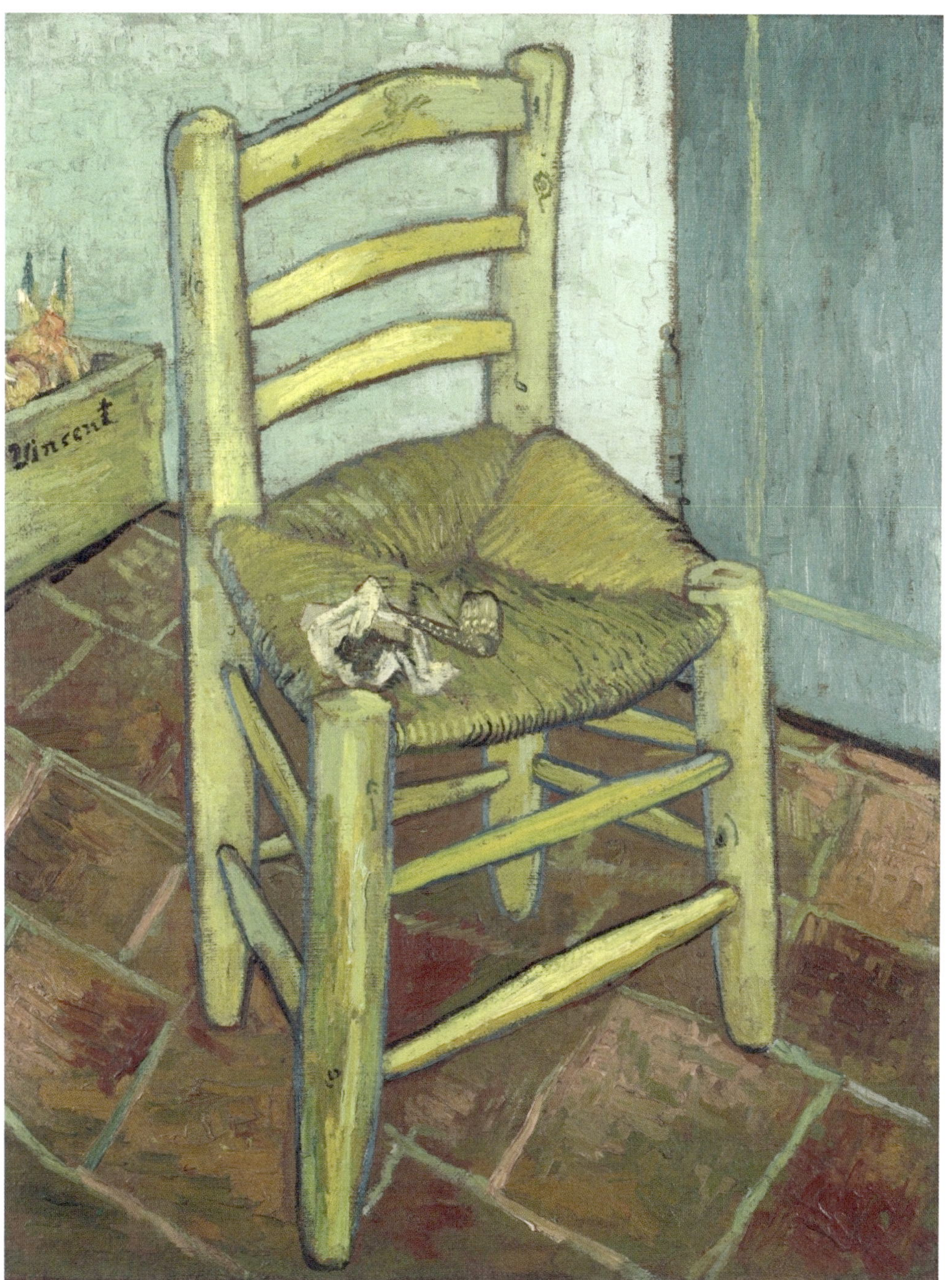
Vincent

So this work was returned to Amsterdam and *Sunflowers* bought instead for £1,304.

In the spring of 1924 the Millbank gallery organised a temporary exhibition of the four newly acquired Van Goghs, plus some loans from Amsterdam, and a few years later they were moved to a place in the permanent collection. However, Van Gogh was still regarded as a dubious figure on the cutting edge. In 1926, Courtauld telephoned Ede to say that the trustees were thinking of buying another Van Gogh painting, and in that case might sell *Van Gogh's Chair* (fig. 27) as there was a danger of having 'too many Van Goghs'. Fortunately, he changed his mind.

Perhaps the National Gallery, Millbank, was following this policy of minimising its array of Van Goghs when it omitted *Sunflowers* from a publication recording over 100 recent important purchases, *A Record of Ten Years 1917–1927*. Eventually, and overwhelmingly, the public took the painting to its heart. In 1961 it was moved from the Millbank gallery, by then renamed the Tate, to the National Gallery on Trafalgar Square. In the twenty-first century, no work in this collection of great masterpieces is more loved and admired than Van Gogh's glorious *Sunflowers*.

There are many reasons why this painting is considered to be one of the most celebrated works of art in the world. Some of these are rooted in its history: Van Gogh himself seems to have regarded this as the culmination of his *Sunflowers* series; others, such as Gauguin, thought this canvas was the quintessence of his art. As we have seen, it is a landmark in art history. But there are other factors, less easy to define, that make it so compelling. One of these, undoubtedly, is its particular combination of intensity and economy. In the National Gallery's *Sunflowers* Van Gogh created an image of his own vitality, love of beauty and of the poignant brevity of passing time. And he did this so directly that almost everyone who sees it senses what he felt that hot, windy August in Arles.

NOTES

1 Thomson 1993, p.99.
2 Jansen and Robert 1999, p.81.
3 Stein 1986, p.121.
4 Letter 653.
5 Letter 574.
6 Naifeh and White Smith 2013, p.208.
7 Conversation with the author.
8 Heron in Zurich 1963, n.p.
9 Letter 575, note 9.
10 Ibid.
11 Letter 856.
12 From Alfred, Lord Tennyson, 'Song: A Spirit Haunts the Year's Last Hours' (1830).
13 Horner 1933, p.119.
14 Letter 667.
15 Jansen and Robert 1999, p.160.
16 See Bailey 2013, p.10.
17 *Still Life with a Plate of Onions*, 1889, Kröller-Müller Museum, Otterlo.
18 Jansen and Robert 1999, pp.121–2.
19 In 1920 the painting was bought by Koyata Yamamoto, a businessman from the town of Ashiya. On 6 August 1945, the day the atomic bomb was dropped on Hiroshima, Ashiya was attacked in a separate raid by the American air force. Yamamoto escaped from his burning house, but there was no time to save the Van Gogh. See Bailey 2013, pp.182–5.
20 Letter 670.
21 Towards the end of his life, while living in Polynesia, Gauguin wrote a strange short story which blurred, altered and blended various characters and incidents from his stay in Arles. The central character was apparently based on the owner of a brothel in Arles, one Louis Farce, with whom Gauguin struck up an acquaintanceship. This narrative, however, was set in the past – the 1870s – and the painter the brothel-keeper gets to know is not Gauguin or Van Gogh, but Manet. The latter made him a present, 'a little study of flowers, two white camellias in a glass of water'. *Diverses choses* (1896–8), manuscript, Cabinet des Dessins, Musée du Louvre, Paris, RF7259.
22 Gayford 2006, p.160.
23 Gauguin 1936, p.33.
24 Nienke Bakker, Senior Curator, Van Gogh Museum, quoted in 'Exhibition shows how Van Gogh's *Sunflowers* looked fresh from the studio', *Dutch News*, 20 June 2019.
25 Letter 677.
26 See Van Tilborgh and Hendriks 2001. It may be that Van Gogh was not happy with the effect of the painting on the jute support, since he did not sign it.
27 Letter from Katherine Mansfield to Dorothy Brett, 5 December 1921, in Middleton Murry 1929, p.423.
28 Bailey 2013, p.105.
29 Middleton Murry 1929, p.423.
30 Bailey 2013, pp.157–62.
31 Letter from Jo van Gogh-Bonger to Charles Aitken, 24 January 1924, Van Gogh Museum, Amsterdam (inv. b5951).
32 Edinburgh 2006, p.25.

FURTHER READING

References to Van Gogh's letters are indicated in the text by numbers in square brackets.

All quotations from the letters are taken from the online edition of Van Gogh's complete correspondence: L. Jansen, H. Lujten and N. Bakker (eds), *Vincent van Gogh: The Letters. The Complete, Illustrated and Annotated Edition*, 6 vols, Amsterdam, The Hague and Brussels 2009, www.vangoghletters.org

Bailey 2013
M. Bailey, *The Sunflowers are Mine: The Story of Van Gogh's Masterpiece*, London 2013

Bakker and Hendriks 2019
N. Bakker and E. Hendriks, *Van Gogh and the Sunflowers: A Masterpiece Examined*, Amsterdam 2019

Chicago 2001
D.W. Druick and P.K. Zegers, *Van Gogh and Gauguin: The Studio of the South*, exh. cat., The Art Institute of Chicago 2001

Edinburgh 2006
M. Bailey, *Van Gogh and Britain: Pioneer Collectors*, exh. cat., National Galleries of Scotland, Edinburgh 2006

Gauguin 1936
P. Gauguin, *Paul Gauguin's Intimate Journals*, trans. V.W. Brooks, New York 1936

Gayford 2006
M. Gayford, *The Yellow House: Van Gogh, Gauguin and Nine Turbulent Weeks in Arles*, London 2006

Horner 1933
F. Horner, *Time Remembered*, London 1933

Jansen and Robert 1999
L. Jansen and J. Robert (eds), *Brief Happiness: The Correspondence of Theo van Gogh and Jo Bonger*, Amsterdam and Zwolle 1999

London 2024–5
C. Homburg et al., *Van Gogh: Poets & Lovers*, exh. cat., The National Gallery, London 2024–5

Middleton Murry 1929
J. Middleton Murry (ed.), *The Letters of Katherine Mansfield*, vol. 2, New York 1929, archive.org/stream/lettersofkatheri031425mbp/lettersofkatheri031425mbp_djvu.txt

Naifeh and White Smith 2013
S. Naifeh and G. White Smith, *Van Gogh: The Life*, New York and London 2013

Stein 1986
S.A. Stein, *Van Gogh: A Retrospective*, New York 1986

Thomson 1993
B. Thomson (ed.), *Gauguin by Himself*, New York and London 1993

Van Tilborgh and Hendriks 2001
L. van Tilborgh and E. Hendriks, 'The Tokyo Sunflowers: A Genuine Repetition by Van Gogh or a Schuffenecker Forgery?', *Van Gogh Museum Journal*, 2001, pp.16–43, www.dbnl.org/tekst/_van012200101_01/index.php

Zurich 1963
P. Heron and J.P. Hodin, *Patrick Heron*, exh. cat., Galerie Charles Lienhard, Zurich 1963

PICTURE CREDITS

© The National Gallery, London: figs 1, 27.

© Van Gogh Museum, Amsterdam (Vincent Van Gogh Foundation): figs 2, 11, 12, 14, 18, 19, 20, 26.

© The Metropolitan Museum of Art/Art Resource/Scala, Florence: fig. 3.

Staatsgemäldesammlungen, Neue Pinakothek, Munich © Photo Scala, Firenze/bpk, Bildagentur für Kunst, Kultur und Geschichte, Berlin: fig. 4.

The J. Paul Getty Museum, Los Angeles, California. Image courtesy of the Getty's Open Content Program: fig. 5.

Kunstmuseum Den Haag © akg-images: fig. 6.

Private Collection © World History Archive / Alamy Stock Photo: fig. 7.

© The Art Institute of Chicago: figs 8, 21.

© Kunstmuseum, Bern: fig. 9.

© The Metropolitan Museum of Art, New York: fig. 10.

Private collection © Courtesy the owner. Photo: Tate: fig. 13.

Private collection © Artepics / Alamy Stock Photo: fig. 15.

Factum Arte. Photo © Oak Taylor-Smith | Factum Arte: fig. 16.

Musée d'Orsay, Paris © RMN-Grand Palais (Musée d'Orsay) / Hervé Lewandowski: fig. 17.

Sompo Museum of Art, Tokyo, Japan © akg-images: fig. 22.

© Museum of Fine Arts, Boston, Massachusetts: fig. 23.

© Philadelphia Museum of Art, Pennsylvania: fig. 24.

© Collection Kröller-Müller Museum, Otterlo, the Netherlands. Photographer: Rik Klein Gotink: fig. 25.

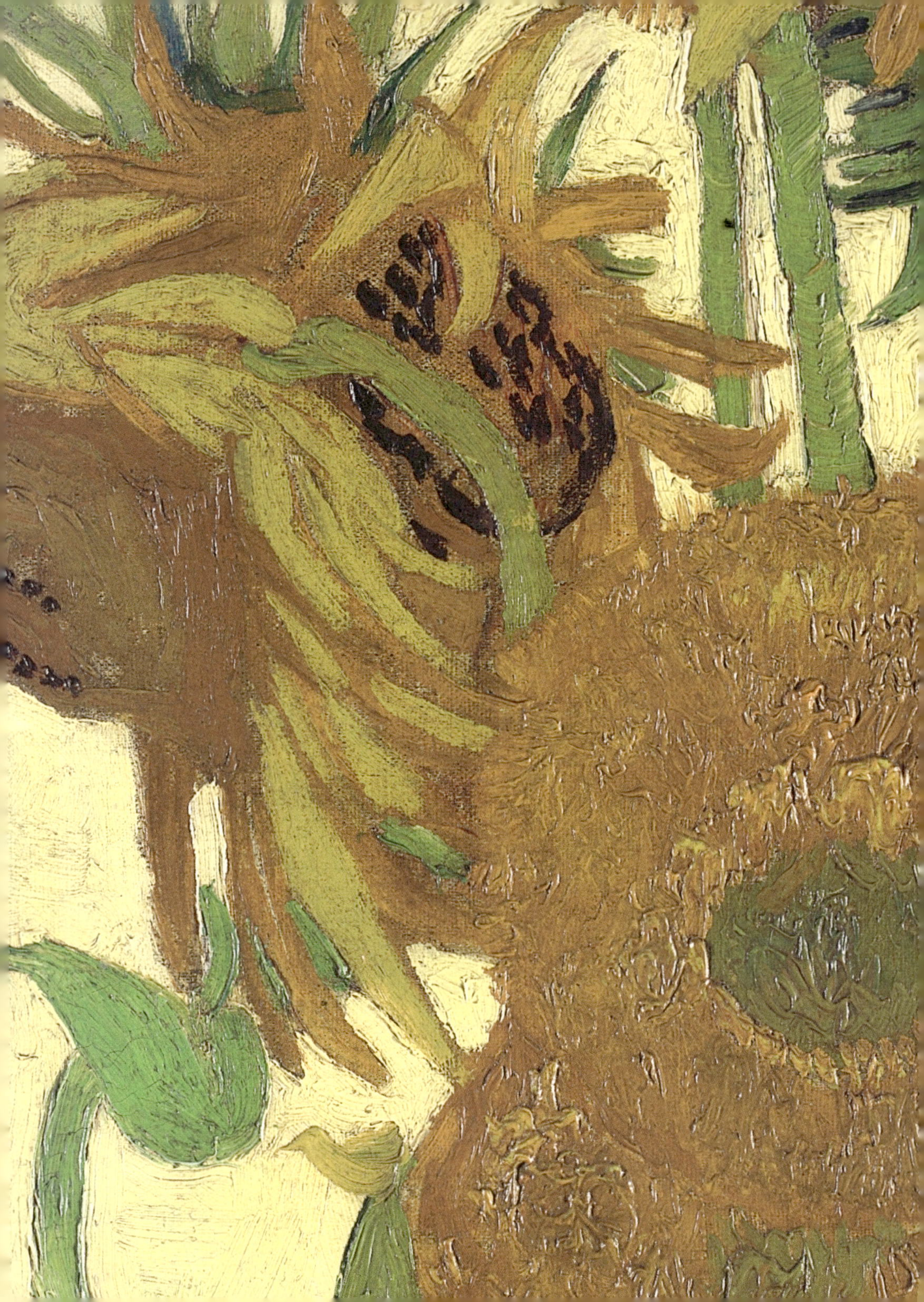

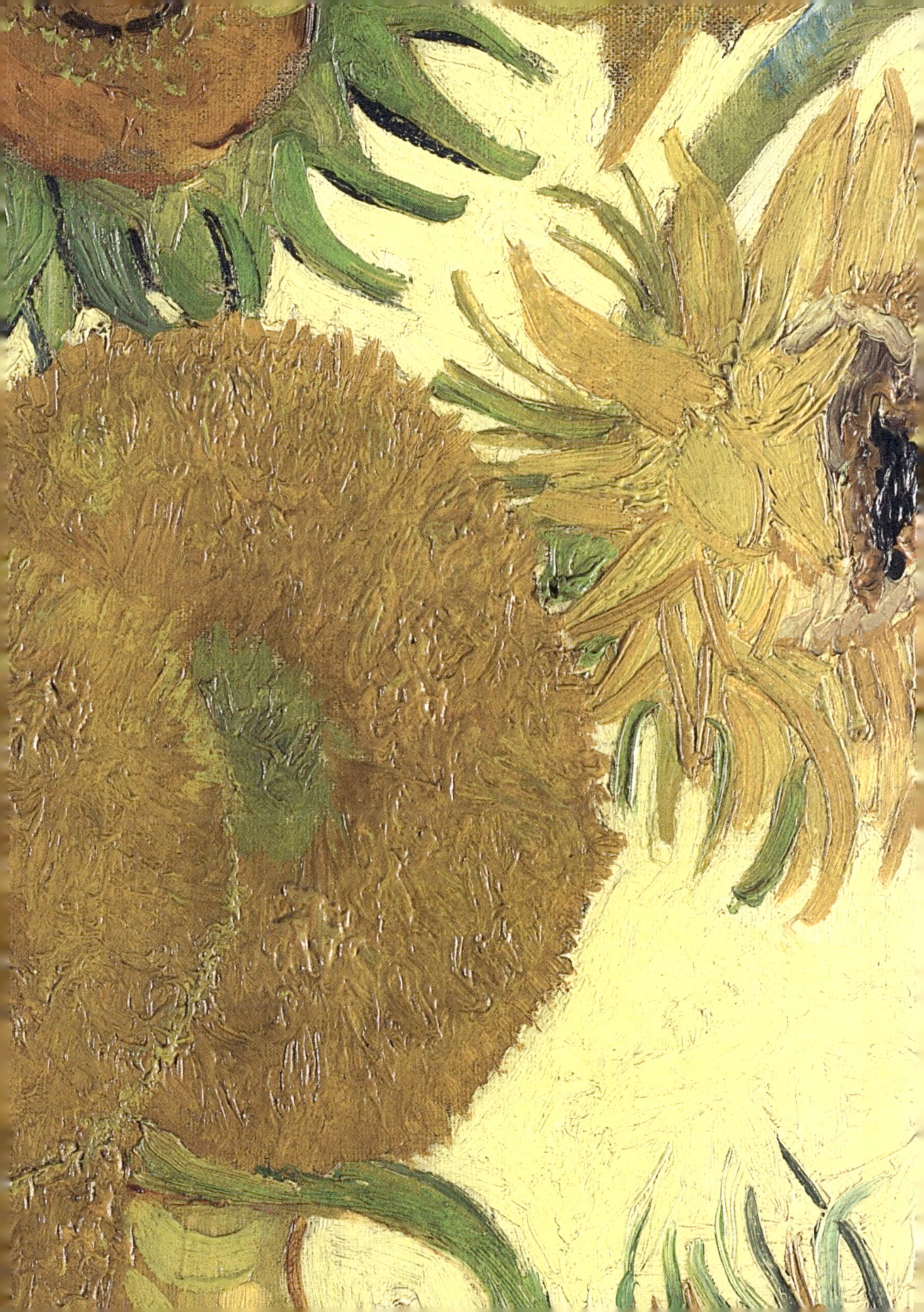

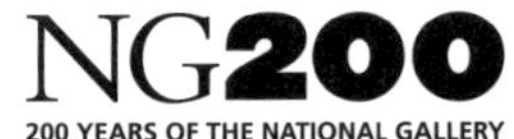

Martin Gayford is a celebrated author and journalist. His publications have ranged from biographical studies of artists including Michelangelo and Constable to volumes on Freud and Hockney. His book *The Yellow House: Van Gogh, Gauguin, and Nine Turbulent Weeks in Arles* was published in 2006 to critical acclaim.

First published in 2024 by
National Gallery Global Limited
Trafalgar Square
London WC2N 5DN
www.shop.nationalgallery.org.uk

ISBN: 978 1 85709 729 0
1053994

British Library Cataloguing-in-Publication Data
A catalogue record is available from the British Library

Publisher: Laura Lappin
Project Editor: Flora Allen
Copy-editor: Kate Bell
Picture Researcher:
Rebecca Thornton
Production: Davina Cheung

Designed by Sandra Zellmer
Origination by DL Imaging, London
Printed in Italy by Printer Trento

All works are by Vincent van Gogh (1853–1890) unless otherwise stated.

All measurements give height before width.

Cover and pp.4, 62–3:
details from Vincent van Gogh, *Sunflowers*, 1888 (fig. 1)

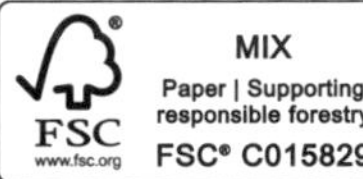